Raising Self-Esteem *in* Adults

by the same author

Mandala Symbolism and Techniques
Innovative Approaches for Professionals
Susan I. Buchalter
ISBN 978 1 84905 889 6
eISBN 978 0 85700 593 9

Art Therapy and Creative Coping Techniques for Older Adults
Susan I. Buchalter
ISBN 978 1 84905 830 8
eISBN 978 0 85700 309 6

Art Therapy Techniques and Applications
Susan I. Buchalter
ISBN 978 1 84905 806 3
eISBN 978 1 84642 961 3

A Practical Art Therapy
Susan I. Buchalter
ISBN 978 1 84310 769 9
eISBN 978 1 84642 004 7

of related interest

Helping Adolescents and Adults to Build Self-Esteem
A Photocopiable Resource Book
2nd edition
Deborah M. Plummer
ISBN 978 1 84905 425 6
eISBN 978 0 85700 794 0

The CBT Art Activity Book
100 illustrated handouts for creative therapeutic work
Jennifer Guest
ISBN 978 1 84905 665 6

Raising Self-Esteem *in* Adults

An Eclectic Approach with Art Therapy, CBT and DBT Based Techniques

SUSAN I. BUCHALTER

Jessica Kingsley *Publishers*
London and Philadelphia

First published in 2015
by Jessica Kingsley Publishers
73 Collier Street
London N1 9BE, UK
and
400 Market Street, Suite 400
Philadelphia, PA 19106, USA

www.jkp.com

Library of Congress Cataloging in Publication Data
A CIP catalog record for this book is available from the Library of Congress

British Library Cataloguing in Publication Data
A CIP catalogue record for this book is available from the British Library

ISBN 978 1 84905 966 4
eISBN 978 0 85700 821 3

"Between stimulus and response, there is a space. In that space lays our freedom and power to choose our response. In our response lies our growth and freedom."

Viktor E. Frankl, Man's Search for Meaning

Dedicated to Alan, Jennifer, Adam,
Alexandra, Josh, Tom and Kathryn.

Contents

Acknowledgments

I would like to thank Dr. Alan H. Katz for his wonderful technical support, and Dr. Marsha Linehan for her graciousness in allowing me to use a variety of DBT ideas and skills, many of which I incorporated with art therapy techniques.

Preface

In order for people to recover from illness they must find a purpose in life and believe that they are worthy of getting well. Self-esteem becomes the first step towards healing; it is the building block of recovery. Once the individual feels worthy the process begins; he will most likely begin attending therapy, taking his medication, and visiting the doctor or therapist. His motivation towards helping himself will increase and he will begin to feel more positive.

Self-esteem may be affected when individuals are challenged with loss, major life changes, disability, and illness, especially psychological illness. It is common for people to believe psychological illness is their fault. They may feel guilty and lose self-worth. Low self-esteem seems to go hand in hand with depression, anxiety disorders, and chemical based illnesses such as bipolar disorder and schizophrenia. The culmination of feeling like a burden, needing extra help, losing certain abilities (even if this is temporary), and possible personality changes, have a negative effect on most individuals. Many people feel shame; in addition they may not receive the appropriate support from their family, friends, and community. Some individuals feel a sense of hopelessness, helplessness, and isolation. When self-esteem is low the individual may actually lose his sense of self. He forgets his strengths, achievements, accomplishments, and positive personality characteristics. He may even forget how important his value is to others. A father, for instance, may not feel worthy of being a father and stop caring for his children and/or interacting with them. He may believe he doesn't deserve them and they would be better off without him in their life. Certain individuals will feel so unworthy that they will stop taking their medications, stop engaging in healthy endeavors like exercising and eating nutritiously, and stop seeing the doctor. They may self-medicate and even resort to taking drugs, drinking, and other self-defeating activities. They will deteriorate and become victims of their distorted thinking. It is a difficult task to increase self-esteem in someone who feels undeserving.

Core beliefs are strongly held beliefs individuals possess, often from childhood. If an individual has negative core beliefs about himself it takes much understanding and self-awareness to begin to transform those beliefs. This publication contains a large variety of techniques that have helped clients learn to become more aware of their core beliefs, emotions, and patterns of behavior. Many of the techniques have motivated clients to change unconstructive attitudes into more positive ones.

The techniques do not work overnight and not every exercise is suitable for every client. Therapists and others reading this publication will need to determine which techniques seem most helpful and doable for each particular person/group. The ultimate goal would be for clients to have as many techniques as possible at their disposal and to use them as needed. This makes the individual stronger and in better control of his life. I like to call the grouping of exercises the "mental toolbox." The individual picks and chooses which tool to use for each confrontation, experience, problem, and mood.

I tend to refer to patients as clients, but I will use the terms interchangeably. I have the utmost respect for the group participants I see on a daily basis, and using these terms is for descriptive purposes. I also use "he" when describing people in generic terms. This is to avoid confusion and allow the writing to flow more readily. As I have stated in my other publications, this is not a cookbook of techniques but an array of ideas to help further enhance the quality of patient work. My objective is to help individuals find ways to increase self-awareness and self-worth, better cope with problems, and ultimately increase their life satisfaction.

Introduction

Self-esteem develops from many sources including one's self-appraisal, achievements, parental support and approval, acceptance by friends and significant people in one's life, and handling of challenges faced throughout the years. "Self-esteem is how we value ourselves; it is how we perceive our value to the world and how valuable we think we are to others."[1] In psychology, the term self-esteem is used to describe a person's overall sense of self-worth or personal value. The Oxford English Dictionary defines self-esteem as confidence in one's own worth. According to Nathaniel Branden, PhD "Self-esteem is the experience of being competent to cope with the basic challenges of life and of being worthy of happiness."[2]

Self-esteem and self-acceptance are two terms that vary slightly, self-acceptance being more internal and self-esteem emanating more from outside sources and perceived judgments. Self-acceptance involves the acknowledgement that an individual is acceptable as he is in the moment, even with possible illness, problems and flaws. It requires the acceptance of everything about oneself. "This is different from self-esteem, which is a measurement of how worthy we see ourselves."[3] The two terms are similar enough that they are used interchangeably in therapy groups and will be used interchangeably in the following chapters.

Ideally someone with healthy self-esteem has mastered self-acceptance and will feel worthwhile just because he is a human being doing his best to get by in the world. He will feel "good enough" regardless of his job, profession, partner, or lack thereof, financial situation, environment, home, etc. All of these things are external and can change with time. If an individual bases his self-worth on external factors, then his self-worth is tenuous and not genuine. On the other hand, if an individual bases his self-esteem on his inherent qualities and uniqueness then it will be stronger, longer lasting and more valuable. It will stand the test of time. Instead of feeling defeated permanently when he experiences loss or defeat, he will usually bounce back quicker and begin anew. He will understand that it is not the failing or falling that is so bad, it is the inability to get back up that is harmful. He will possess the ego strength to start a project, relationship, job, etc. once again.

Positive self-esteem can help clients heal quicker. It provides individuals with the impetus to fight, to struggle for a better existence. It is the building block of wellness. There are so many factors that contribute to one's self-esteem. These factors might include: family, friends, teachers, environment, skills, physical abilities, varied experiences, and relationships, etc. As children and young adults we have less power, but as adults we can work towards developing greater self-awareness and changing negative thought patterns. Our thinking plays a huge role in our decisions regarding who we are and what type of person we'd like to become in the future. In essence, we define ourselves.

The goals of the exercises included in the following chapters aim to enhance a feeling of self-awareness and self-esteem. Each exercise tackles this subject in a different but meaningful manner. The more techniques we have at our fingertips to enhance our feelings of worthiness the stronger and more in control we will be. Creative writing, art, and music all play a role in our ability to accept ourselves and to put our energies into creating goals instead of self-defeating thoughts and behaviors.

Cognitive behavioral therapy (CBT) supports individuals to become aware of core beliefs, which may help or impede their self-esteem. Clients examine erroneous thinking patterns that can harm their self-worth and outlook on life. They learn how certain patterns of thinking and behavior can lower self-esteem and depress mood. The therapy involves the teaching of methods to transform negative thoughts into more positive thoughts so that people can become more optimistic about their goals, personal characteristics, and relationships. CBT enables individuals to understand the strong relationship between their thoughts, emotions, and resulting behaviors. It helps them improve their quality of life.

Dialectical behavioral therapy helps people become increasingly mindful. They practice how to be in the moment, "stop and smell the roses," and appreciate their life. They learn not to judge themselves and others, and how to better relate to others. Individuals practice how to regulate their emotions while validating themselves and their life. Focus is placed on the understanding of the emotional, reasonable, and wise mind. The exploration of the benefits of using one's wise mind, which aids in greater self-awareness and positive functioning, is an important skill. Individuals learn techniques to cope with fear, frustration, and anger.

Art therapy provides individuals with the opportunity to focus on their strengths in a creative manner. They create their own environment and personal world in their artwork. The artist is the master of his universe, often choosing his own themes, colors, shapes, materials, and images. The art therapist encourages individuals not to judge themselves, to let their work flow. Participants learn that self-expression becomes the most important aspect of creative work. The art doesn't have to be perfect; each person's designs are unique. The concept, that we are allowed to experiment and make mistakes, is crucial in the development of self-esteem. When individuals acknowledge that they don't have to be perfect, they are better able to accept their perceived flaws and "themselves as a whole." They are often able to identify and focus on strengths instead of weaknesses.

Self-esteem is crucial for a healthy and happy existence and successful relationships. It helps individuals deal with illness, loss, stress, and unpleasant experiences. Self-esteem encourages people to take care of themselves physically as well as psychologically, and to take healthy risks such as standing up for themselves, applying for a new job, moving away from home for the first time, getting married, or going to college. A good sense of self-esteem can be considered a learned skill that needs nurturing and practice. It helps people better cope and increases happiness in all phases of their life.

NOTES

1. www.ucdmc.ucdavis.edu/hr/hrdepts/asap/Documents/Self_esteem.pdf
2. http://nathanielbranden.com/on-self-esteem, accessed on 9 October, 2014.
3. http://science.howstuffworks.com/life/happy-with-yourself1.htm, accessed on 9 October, 2014.

CHAPTER 1

Art Therapy

Engaging in art therapy allows the client the opportunity to communicate thoughts, feelings, concerns, problems, wishes, hopes, dreams, and desires in a relatively non-threatening manner. The artwork serves as a safe vehicle to express unconscious as well as conscious issues and beliefs. Creative expression through art provides the individual with the freedom to represent his inner and outer world in any way he chooses. There are no judgments and the client is told that however he chooses to draw is perfectly acceptable. The individual is informed that he may use stick figures, lines, colors, shapes, abstractions, or realism to portray his thoughts. A variety of materials such as markers, oil pastels, crayons, and various sizes of drawing paper are presented. In this way clients can decide which materials to use. Decision making is very important; it helps enhance problem-solving skills, and increases independence and self-esteem.

Art promotes creative expression and release of emotions. It helps reduce stress while increasing self-awareness and self-esteem. Healing begins as the artist gains a better perspective of his problems and concerns. Energy is expended in a healthy manner while meaningful images and symbols are created. A catharsis or release is frequently experienced while clients become focused and involved in the artwork. Self-esteem increases due to a sense of accomplishment and the completion of a project from start to finish. Strengths the individual never knew he had are discovered and then relished for years to come. The artist is in control and creates the rules. Art allows us to "draw from within" and express ourselves in our own unique manner. Benefits of art therapy include:

- expressing and sharing inner experiences in a visual way

- acquiring healthy creative outlets for intense feelings

- reducing stress and learning creative stress management techniques

- sharing problems and concerns through artistic expression

- experimenting and learning how to use a variety of media

- developing self-awareness and identifying areas of concern

- developing talents and acknowledging strengths (some of which have been long forgotten)

- being valued as part of a community that fosters non-judgment and acceptance.

Taking time to discuss the artwork allows clients to observe, analyze, and relate to representations and figures illustrated. It provides for group interaction and feedback from others. Group members are able to reflect on the symbols drawn, and thoughts may be conveyed that would otherwise not be shared verbally. The artwork serves as a compilation of feelings, problems, concerns, and solutions that are exclusively the client's own. Images serve as vehicles, which facilitates communication, growth, and insight.

HONOR

Materials: Drawing paper, markers, oil pastels, pen, and pencils.

Procedure: Have clients complete the following sentence: "I honor myself because…" Next ask them to draw a symbol that would demonstrate how they might show admiration for themselves and/ or why they deserve a tribute (for example being a good parent, a good friend, intelligent, a college graduate, good cook, etc.).

A circle might be used to help clients structure their work if desired. They can trace it from a paper plate and place their symbol inside it. Examples of possible symbols: an award, a trophy, star, jewelry, heart, smiling face, flowers, a banner, a medal, applause (hands clapping), etc.

Discussion: Clients share their representations and achievements. Goals include increased self-esteem and identification of strengths.

GRATITUDE I

Materials: Drawing paper, scissors, glue, magazine photos, markers, oil pastels, and crayons.

Procedure: Ask group members to "express gratitude to their body." They may draw their response and/or use magazine photos, words, and phrases.

Discussion: Participants explore strengths and abilities. Individuals become aware of the simple pleasures in life that most people take for granted (e.g. tasting, walking, touching, hearing music, experiencing life, seeing a sunset, hugging a loved one, etc.).

POSITIVE AND NEGATIVE

Materials: Drawing paper, markers, pencils, and pens.

Procedure: Have clients outline a head and divide it in half. Suggest that facial features may be added if desired. Ask group members to fill in one side with positive thoughts (e.g. I am worthy, I am smart, etc.) and the other side with negative thoughts (e.g. I am weak, I will never get well, etc.).

Discussion: Encourage clients to explore how their self-talk affects their mood, behavior, and recovery. Discuss the idea that "we decide much of the course of our life and level of happiness by the way we process our thoughts, the way we choose to think about our ourselves and our circumstances." Goals include self-awareness and re-examination of the messages we are sending and receiving.

SPIRAL OF HOPE

Materials: Drawing paper, pens, pencils, colored pencils, and markers.

Procedure: Provide a large spiral (should take up most of the page) with approximately ¾ inch (2 cm) space in-between the lines that create the spiral. Divide the spiral rings every 2 inches. Ask clients to fill in the spaces with colors, symbols, words and phrases, and affirmations of hope.

Discussion: Discuss the meaning of the symbols, words, and phrases that are included in the spirals. Explore how the spiral shape may relate to our thoughts and feelings. Goals include representation of hope, attitude, mood, and direction in life.

BOWL OF HAPPINESS

Materials: Pens, pencils, markers, colored pencils, oil pastels and crayons, and a pre-drawn bowl on sheets of paper (or clients may draw their own bowl).

Procedure: Direct clients to fill their bowl in with color according to how much happiness they have in their life. Discuss the amount of happiness in each bowl and explore the following:

1. Is your bowl filled with enough happiness?
2. Will it last?
3. When was the last time the bowl was full?
4. When was the last time, if ever, it was empty?
5. What is "real happiness"?

6. How does attitude affect happiness?

7. How do relationships affect happiness?

8. Are there special habits or rituals that can add to happiness (e.g. praying, planting and taking care of flowers, talking to a family member each day)?

9. How does reaching out and helping others affect happiness?

10. How do you/can you create your own happiness?

Discussion: Discussion focuses on examining ways to increase life satisfaction and acquire a more positive attitude. Goals include increased self-esteem and greater awareness of our responsibility for our own happiness.

HAPPINESS I

Materials: Copies of a sheet with a variety of pre-drawn keys on it, scissors, glue, drawing paper, markers, pens, pencils, oil pastels, and crayons. Pictures may be found on Google Images or elsewhere on the Internet.

Procedure: Discuss the meaning of the phrase "The key to happiness." Next have group members choose a variety of the keys, cut and color them in, and then glue them on the drawing paper. Have group members write what they think "the key to happiness is" inside the keys or beside them.

Discussion: Discussion focuses on the number of keys chosen and the ideas presented. Goals include problem solving and exploration of coping skills.

GRATITUDE: TREASURE CHEST

Materials: Copies of a pre-drawn picture of a treasure chest, pens and pencils, and markers.

Procedure: Ask clients to decorate the treasure chest and fill it in with everything they are thankful for in their life (examples include children, friends, health, rainbows, food, a home, etc.).

Discussion: Clients share their treasures and discuss the importance of their positive experiences. Goals include emphasis on optimistic thinking and increased self-esteem.

SAYING "NO"

"Saying no to others is saying yes to yourself."[1]

Materials: Drawing paper, scissors, glue, magazines, markers, pens, pencils, oil pastels, and crayons.

Procedure: Participants write the word "No" on the paper. Then they surround the "No" with images that represent strength, power, and being in control.

Examples of drawings and photos may include:

- a lion

- someone with his arms crossed

- weight lifter

- someone running, exercising

- a person defending another person

- police officer

- King/Queen

- warrior.

Discussion: Explore the benefits of being assertive. Examine the differences between being assertive, aggressive, and passive-aggressive. Discuss how saying "No" allows for increased self-esteem and greater psychological growth. Discuss the importance of boundary and limit setting.

SELF-ESTEEM TOWER

Materials: Drawing paper, markers, oil pastels, and magazine photos.

Procedure: Participants are instructed to create a tower of methods to enhance feelings of self-worth. They may design it using markers and/or pastels and add magazine photos if desired. They may use line, shape, form, and color to create their own unique image.

Discussion: Clients share their constructions and specifically what they need to increase their self-esteem. They examine realistic goals and methods to attain them.

Questions such as: "What type of environment do you need to feel content?" and "What type of relationships do you need in your life?" may be explored. Discuss the size and shape of the tower as well as the sturdiness or frailty of it. Determine how long the tower has been in existence and the timetable for future growth.

Examples of items that may be included as part of the tower: pets, children, smiling faces, people exercising, people helping each other, affirmations, people engaged in sports and games, and families.

CHANGING IMAGES

Materials: Drawing paper, markers, oil pastels, and crayons.

Procedure: Participants draw an image representing a negative feeling or action. Next they "edit the image." They either draw over the original image or create a new image to make it more positive.

Discussion: Participants examine ways to *edit* their own negative thoughts, attitudes and behaviors in order to think more optimistically.

SELF-ESTEEM BUCKET

Materials: Markers, oil pastels, pens, pencils, and an outline of a bucket that fills an 8½ × 11 inch (21 × 28 cm) sheet of paper.

Procedure: The leader provides each client with an outline of a bucket. The bucket may be hand drawn or taken from Google Images. Clients are asked to decorate the bucket and fill it in with color. Inform group members that the amount of color they use to fill it will represent their degree of self-esteem.

Discussion: Clients will observe if their bucket is full, half full, moderately full or empty. They will relate this presentation to their feelings of self-worth. Questions to ask include:

- Are there holes in the bucket? If so, how many? What could the holes mean in terms of self-esteem?

- Were there fewer holes in the past?

- Is there a way to patch the holes?

The holes will relate to loss of self-esteem. Goals include identifying reasons for poor self-esteem and exploration of ways to increase it.

TOTEM POLE

Materials: Drawing paper, markers, paint, magazine photos, glue, scissors, oil pastels, pens, pencils, and crayons.

Procedure: Suggest that clients create a totem pole of positive images (to represent their strengths, achievements, and attributes). Encourage them to think about the size, width, color, and strength of the tower. Affirmations and positive words may be included. When it is completed ask them to list their strengths and achievements next to it.

Examples of strengths include: friendly, smart, loyal, polite, funny, good natured, good parent, good grandparent, wonderful cook, sincere, organized, artistic, creative, energetic, relaxed, patient, curious, persistent, willing to take healthy risks, honest, and trustworthy.

Discussion: Clients examine the relationship between the totem pole and their feelings of self-worth. Goals include identifying attitudes, self-talk, and positive attributes.

MASKS

Materials: Paint, brushes, magazines, scissors, glue, Mod Podge[2] (PVA),tissue paper, collage materials such as buttons, feathers, sequins, glitter, and cut paper.

Procedure: Provide clients with masks and suggest they decorate them in their own unique style. Suggest they create a mask that reflects qualities they like about themselves (e.g. a large smile would reflect a sense of humor). Next have them paint the masks, and then add collage materials if desired. Clients may also create collage masks using small pieces of magazine photos or tissue paper glued onto the masks and then painted with Mod Podge or varnish.

Discussion: Group members share ways in which the masks reflect various aspects of their personality. Goals include decision-making, self-expression and exploration of self-image. Clients will be asked to focus on positive qualities.

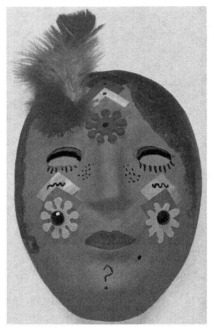

FIGURE 1

Maria, a 41-year-old client diagnosed with bipolar disorder, designed this striking mask. She used a combination of materials including paint, feathers, markers, sequins, colored stones, and shiny paper squares. It was difficult for her to focus at first because she wanted to use all the materials presented immediately. She needed structure and was asked to take a deep breath and focus on using one item at a time. As she worked Maria remarked that the mask was a reminder of the times she put on her own "personal mask." She stated that she attempts to control her emotions when she is with others but sometimes feels pressured and stressed while doing so, "because it takes a lot of energy for me to maintain control." She felt the mask, although bright and cheerful, had a rigidity to it that wasn't representative of her true personality. In reality she was very lively and outgoing, bordering on flamboyant. Her radical mood swings had been a problem for her for many years.

Maria appeared pleased that the mask was very pretty and she mentioned that she often felt beautiful and was admired by both men and women. She viewed her appearance as both a benefit and a hindrance. The benefit was that people "did her favors" and were friendly albeit in a superficial manner. Once people got to know her they began "judging her." She remarked that she couldn't live up to the high expectations her family, husband, and friends had of her. Maria felt the needed to be perfect and her self-esteem dropped when she realized she "had flaws."

Maria shared that the mask represented her creative side and that it symbolized her desire to enjoy life to the fullest. The question mark on the chin represented her inability to decide which direction her life was going in. She wanted to go back to school to become a dental hygienist but she wasn't sure she could focus on the courses she would need to complete to obtain the certification. Maria shared that she enjoyed designing the mask and felt it was calming, and gave her the opportunity to address her feelings about herself and her goals.

STOP SIGN I

Materials: Drawing paper, markers, pens, collage materials such as sequins, buttons, felt, etc., pencils, and oil pastels.

Procedure: Clients are asked to draw an eye-catching stop sign. They may decorate it with markers, paint, sequins, buttons, etc.

Discussion: Discuss the acronym STOPP[3] and how it helps when stressed, anxious and/or using distorted thinking such as catastrophizing (magnifying situations so that they seem much worse than they are in reality):

S—Stop and Step Back: Try not to act on impulse; assess the situation.

T—Take a Breath: Take a Breath and think about your feelings and reactions to what is occurring.

O—Observe: Try to see the whole picture and put things into perspective.

P—Pull Back: Think about whether your feelings are indeed facts or your individual assessment (personal bias) of the situation. Remember feelings are not necessarily facts. "If you don't ask, you don't know."

P—Practice what works: Explore what is the best course of action. What is the healthiest way for you to handle the situation?

JOYFUL ENVIRONMENT

Materials: Magazines, pastels, oil pastels, markers, glue, drawing paper 9 × 12 inches and/or 12 × 16 inches (30 × 40 cm), magazines, outlines of figures and scissors.

Procedure: Clients are given pre-drawn outlines of figures or they may choose to draw the figure freehand. Next they are instructed to create a positive environment surrounding the figure. Magazine photos, sketches, colors and shapes, words and phrases may be incorporated into the environment. They may include items such as hearts, flowers, trees, animals, people they adore and so on.

Discussion: Participants share ways in which the figure reflects them and how the environment presented is representative of their life as it is now or how they would like it to be in the future. Clients are encouraged to explore and assess the love and happiness in their life, and to be grateful for what they have and experience on a daily basis.

INNER BEAUTY

Materials: Drawing paper, construction paper, magazine photos, glue, scissors, markers, oil pastels, and crayons.

Procedure: Ask clients to draw or create a collage of their "inner beauty." What would it look like? What colors, shapes, lines, figures, photos would represent it? They may sketch, paint, draw and/or use magazine photos to represent it. Examples of photos, colors, or sketches to use: hearts, flowers, a sun shining, children, the ocean, rivers, lakes or streams, colors such as pink, red, light blue, family scenes, sunsets, rainbows, butterflies, mountains, landscapes, a still life, baby animals, personal abstract designs, shapes, lines and figures, and so on.

Discussion: Group members explore their strengths, goodness, honesty, and integrity. Self-awareness about what is really important in life and the beauty of the soul and spirit is focused upon.

WARRIOR

Materials: Markers, oil pastels, and drawing paper.

Procedure: Encourage clients to think about a warrior's traits, for example strong, rises to challenges, tries to right wrongs, determined, takes healthy risks, skillful, loyal, brave, and disciplined. A warrior "gets back on the horse" when he falls. Awareness is a very important trait of the "spiritual warrior."

Next suggest participants draw themselves as a warrior in any way they please. They can use forms, figures, and/or draw the feeling they would experience as a warrior.

Discussion: Explore strengths and skills. Discuss ways in which participants handle obstacles in life. Examine how it feels to be a warrior versus someone who takes a passive role in life. Encourage participants to share ways in which they relate to the figure they drew. Which positive qualities are they able to identify with? Which characteristics do they view as assets?

ART EMPTYING

Materials: Markers, oil pastels, colored pencils, and drawing paper.

Procedure: Ask clients without giving it much thought to begin drawing images, shapes, figures, doodles and so on until the paper is filled or almost filled.

Discussion: Discussion focuses on the exploration of the colors, shapes, and images and the clients' associations to them. Ask clients to focus on the figures that represent something positive about their personality and/or life. Share thoughts regarding release of creativity and the ability to create a meaningful piece of art without worrying about intent or ability. Explore ways to experiment and take healthy risks creatively and in everyday life. Discuss the positives of "letting go" and of "play" in one's life.

INSPIRATION

Materials: Drawing paper, markers, oil pastels, and crayons.

Procedure: Ask clients to illustrate one item, thought, feeling or affirmation that helps get them through the day. Examples might include a morning cup of coffee or tea, a phone call from a family member or reciting an affirmation such as "Taking one day at a time."

Discussion: Discussion focuses on motivation, strengths and attitudes. Goals include expanding clients' repertoire of coping techniques.

HEALING ENERGY

Materials: Drawing paper, markers, oil pastels, crayons, and pastels.

Procedure: Suggest clients attempt to draw "Healing Energy." Ask: "What might it look like? How do you think it feels? Think about colors, shapes, and movement."

Discussion: Discussion focuses on the type of energy portrayed and its meaning for the client. Goals include a focus on power, control, healing, and thinking positively.

FIGURE 2

John, a man in his 60s diagnosed with bipolar disorder, shared that the colors represented his happiness and hope for a brighter future. The movement reflected the positive changes he was making in his life and his hope for acceptance by peers and acquaintances. He remarked that he viewed his life as moving forward and his main goals were to travel and find a soul mate. He had just announced that he liked both men and women and didn't want to be judged. He shared that he felt a sense of freedom by sharing his sexual preferences and he decided he wouldn't let anyone judge him or berate his ideas or activities.

RE-CHARGE

Materials: Drawing paper, markers, oil pastels, pastels, and crayons.

Procedure: Ask clients to draw the way they "re-charge" (the way they gain energy and improve their attitude). For example do they walk, exercise, meditate, get a good night's sleep or swim?

Discussion: Discussion focuses on the drawings and symbols drawn that represent renewal. Goals include exploring methods to energize and inspire.

LUCKY CHARM

Materials: Drawing paper, oil pastels, markers, and crayons.

Procedure: Ask clients to draw their lucky charm. Examples might include a four-leaf clover, horseshoe necklace, rabbit's foot, child or grandchild, special number, religious symbol, ring and so on.

Discussion: Clients share positive thoughts and the good fortune they have had in the past. Goals include thinking optimistically, exploring gratitude and affection, and hope for the future.

RAINBOW TREE

Materials: Drawing paper, markers, oil pastels, and crayons.

Procedure: Direct clients to create their own unique "rainbow tree." Encourage them to think about what they would find at the end of the rainbow or at the top of the tree.

Discussion: Clients share the type of tree depicted and the way it might represent their hope for the future, and their present mood and attitude. Goals include exploration of mood and feeling, and a focus on optimism and positive thinking.

POWER THINKING

Materials: Drawing paper, markers, crayons, and oil pastels.

Procedure: Suggests clients use lines and shapes to represent positive thoughts and healthy thinking (for example, being flexible, accepting change, being patient, taking one day at a time, accepting oneself, not filtering or catastrophizing, etc.).

Discussion: Clients share their shapes and their "thinking strength." Explore the importance of strengthening thinking in order to increase self-esteem, vigor, motivation, and hope.

PASSION

Materials: Drawing paper, markers, oil pastels, and crayons.

Procedure: Suggest that clients draw things they are passionate about. Examples may include children/grandchildren, pets, hobbies, work, art, volunteer positions, sports such as golf and so on.

Discussion: Discussion focuses on the importance of having a passion and/or a purpose in life. Explain the benefits:

- Individuals are generally more positive.
- They often have higher self-esteem and less depression.
- They have more energy.
- They are more likely to fight off disease and illness.
- They live longer.
- They stay younger and think younger.
- They are more exciting and enjoyable to be with.
- Boredom is rarely an issue.
- Having a passion makes it easier to start the day; there is a reason to get up in the morning.

Goals include exploring and developing new hobbies and interests and resuming activities that clients once found fulfilling.

TINY VICTORIES

Materials: Drawing paper, markers, oil pastels, and crayons.

Procedure: Have clients fold their paper in fourths and ask them to fill in the squares with small achievements. Examples may include learning how to cook or sew, getting a driver's license or learning new coping techniques to help decrease anxiety.

Discussion: Encourage clients to share their victories and associated feelings. Discuss the importance of acknowledging good work; emphasize, "Small successes are significant." Goals include increased self-esteem and a focus on strengths.

GOING WITH THE FLOW

Materials: Drawing paper, writing paper, markers, oil pastels, crayons, pens, and pencils.

Procedure: Discuss the meaning of the phrase "Going with the Flow." Generally it means not to resist what happens naturally, to conform, to move along in a specified manner, to act in accordance or harmony, to travel along.

Next read the Taoist story:

A Taoist story tells of an old man who accidentally fell into the river rapids leading to a high and dangerous waterfall. Onlookers feared for his life. Miraculously, he came out alive and unharmed downstream at the bottom of the falls. People asked him how he managed to survive. "I accommodated myself to the water, not the water to me. Without thinking, I allowed myself to be shaped by it. Plunging into the swirl, I came out of the swirl. This is how I survived."

Ask clients their reactions to the story and then have them draw themselves in a swirl of emotion or in a swirl of problems. They may represent themselves and the swirl in any way they please.

Discussion: Clients share their swirl and their connection to it. Questions to ponder include:

- How enmeshed are they in their emotions/problems?

- Do they try to fight their feelings and circumstances or do they work through them and accept life's changes?

- Are they able to view life as a process?

Goals include self-awareness and exploration of coping skills.

THE GOLDEN EGG

Materials: Drawing paper, markers, oil pastels, and crayons.

Procedure: Discuss the meaning of the golden egg. In yoga practices it often means being enlightened, the supreme highest self. One's inner voice that is always calm and perfect, and connected to "the true self." Next ask clients to draw a golden egg or an enlightened figure/symbol of themselves.

Discussion: Clients discuss their associations to the egg and/or figure. Ask them to share the type, size, and color of the egg or symbol. Goals include self-awareness and exploration of ways to attain inner peace and knowledge.

This directive was going to be introduced as a brief warm-up, but it became an hour-long project because clients enjoyed drawing and exploring the images and their meanings. Group members became focused and relaxed as they filled in the eggs with color. When the eggs were completed there was much bantering back and forth. Group members playfully teased each other, making statements like, "My egg is more colorful than your egg; my egg is brighter; my egg looks more like an egg than yours." One client told another client her egg looked like a kitsch hat or perhaps an over done Easter egg.

INNER BEAUTY

Materials: Drawing paper, markers, and oil pastels.

Procedure: Suggest that clients draw their "inner beauty." Ask them, "What would it look like? What colors, shapes, lines would compose it?" Next ask them to write a few words to describe the images.

Discussion: As individuals age their outer beauty often fades but their inner beauty remains. It is important for clients to acknowledge their inner beauty in order to raise self-esteem and to help them focus on their special qualities and what is really important in life.

STRENGTH/AFFIRMATION TREE

Materials: An outline of a bare tree (with a variety of branches and large leaves on it) for each group member, oil pastels crayons, markers, and colored pencils.

Procedure: Have clients decorate the tree and fill in the leaves with positive thoughts and statements.

Discussion: Explore the range of decorative effects and strengths written on the leaves. Goals include awareness of coping skills, positive self-talk, increased self-esteem and acknowledgement of achievements.

EMOTIONS MANDALAS

Materials: Manila folders, markers, oil pastels, crayons, and a coffee can.

Procedure: Instruct clients to outline a circle, using the bottom of the coffee can as a template, on the outside and inside of the folder. Ask group members to fill the outside circle with colors, shapes, figures, and/or a design that would represent a specific emotion. Have them represent the opposite emotion on the inside circle.

Discussion: Discussion focuses on the expression of feelings and concerns. Goals include examining methods to effectively communicate emotions and reconcile conflicts.
Examples of opposites:

- happy—sad

- anxious—calm

- irritable—easy going

- fear—confidence

- brave—cowardly

- hostile—peaceful
- loving—hateful.

A variation of these mini mandalas might include "Life Mandalas." Here clients would fill in the first mandala with colors and shapes that represent their "present life—life as it is now" and the inside mandala would represent "past life—life as it used to be." Here you might discuss differences between past and present life style and environment. Goals would include exploration of the past and present, acceptance, and attitude toward change.

THE APEX

Materials: Drawing paper, markers, oil pastels, crayons, pens, and pencils.

Procedure: Ask clients to draw a mountain and place themselves on top of it. Then ask them to write about a time they reached a goal and/or "felt on top of the world."

Discussion: Discussion focuses on achievements and high points in one's life. Goals include increased self-esteem and review of strengths and accomplishments.

WEED GARDEN

Materials: Drawing paper, construction paper, markers, oil pastels, crayons, scissors, and masking tape.

Procedure: Instruct clients to draw a series of weeds and inside each weed write a negative thought. Have them cut out the weeds from the drawing paper, and using masking tape, have them tape the weeds to the construction paper. Suggest clients create a garden of weeds. As the discussion begins ask clients to begin pulling the weeds (negative thoughts) they want to eliminate out of their garden.

Discussion: Discussion focuses on the type of garden, the number of weeds and the specific weeds pulled. Questions to ponder might include:

- How long ago were the weeds planted?
- Who planted them?
- How did they grow?
- How strong are the weeds?
- How many weeds are there?
- How will you get rid of the weeds?
- How do the weeds affect your life?
- What will replace the weeds?

Goals include self-awareness and examination of methods to stop negative thought patterns.

HAND COLLAGE

Materials: Construction paper, drawing paper, pencils, markers, oil pastels, crayons, glue, scissors, and magazines.

Procedure: Direct clients to outline their hands and then fill the outlines in with self-representative photos from magazines.

Discussion: Discussion focuses on the pictures chosen and their meaning to the client. Goals include sharing likes and dislikes with others (greater communication and socialization), self-awareness, and increase of self-esteem.

HEALING MANDALA COLLAGE

Materials: Drawing paper, markers, magazines, glue, scissors, and paper plates.

Procedure: Have clients create a circle by outlining a paper plate. Direct them to fill in the circle with photos that represent ways in which they are healing. They may add figures, phrases, and words. Examples may include a sun to represent increased energy and happiness, flowers to symbolize beauty, and a river to represent serenity.

Discussion: Discussion focuses on the photos, words, and symbols chosen. Encourage clients to share their feelings and reactions to the collage, and ask them whether or not it is self-representative. Support group members to title the collage and explain the reason/s for the title. Goals include identifying objectives, positive feelings, needs, and ways to gain support.

Most clients chose to represent things that made them feel joyful as opposed to specific healing representations. They were supported to "go with the theme" in any way they chose. Group members appeared very relaxed and focused when working on this directive. The healing came from the actual choosing of the photos, cutting, and gluing as well as processing the completed work.

FIGURE 3

Sarah, a client in her 30s overcoming a severe depression, created a mandala composed mainly of positive words and affirmations. The background is pink to represent her favorite color and "the color of love." The tiny sequins and stones sprinkled within the circle represent her family members (children, husband, parents, aunt, uncle, sisters, and brother). She included words and phrases such as "cook and celebrations" to symbolize her culinary skills and joy of family and life. She also focused on words like motivation, mood lifting, and healthy living. When asked, Sarah remarked that the most important part of the mandala were the words love and mother. She remarked that she takes pride in being a mother and adores her two young children. She stated they give her hope and the motivation to get well and function like she used to before the depression. "The hardest part of being depressed was not being there for my children; I felt so hopeless and guilty. If it wasn't for them it would be difficult to do anything, even to get out of bed in the morning." Sarah shared that she was going to put a backing on this mandala and hang it in her kitchen to inspire her each day.

RE-DEFINING HAPPINESS

Materials: Drawing paper, markers, crayons, oil pastels, and drawing paper.

Procedure: Explore the process of change and the way we adjust to life's circumstances. Discuss how our definition of happiness may need to be transformed during different periods of our life depending on our age, situation, and experiences. Loss of a loved one or long-time job, for instance, may push us to recreate another way of finding joy and fulfillment. After the group discussion ask clients to draw how they can re-define their happiness.

Discussion: Discuss ways to find joy in small pleasures and methods to make transformations. Goals include being mindful and making the most of what we have at the moment.

CONNECTIONS I

Materials: Mural paper, scissors, glue, construction paper, and markers.

Procedure: Ask clients to cut out colorful strips of paper in varying sizes. Next ask them to create a design where their strips interconnect with other group members' strips so that all the pieces are linked in some way and an abstract design is formed.

Discussion: Discussion focuses on connecting with others. Goals include socialization, problem solving, and cooperation among group members.

CONNECTIONS II

Materials: Large sheet of cardboard, markers, oil pastels, scissors, glue sticks, and various outlines of figures.

Procedure: Each client is asked to fill in the outline of at least one or two figures. They may add a face, hair, clothes, etc. or just color and design. Next they carefully cut out the figure and take turns gluing the figures one by one onto the cardboard. Everyone in the group must approve the placement of each figure. After all the figures are glued clients decide what type of background would best illustrate the theme of connections.

Discussion: Participants share their figure/s, the significance of its placement and how they feel about the overall design. The theme of cooperation, respect, and being part of a group is explored.

FIGURE 4

It took three separate sessions for clients to complete this bright and busy mural. Every group member, even those individuals who were usually more withdrawn, participated with gusto. Everyone wanted to contribute and be part of the "group portrait." When participants were asked to discuss the mural they remarked, "The people represent us; they all have smiling faces. They are happy because they are united in togetherness. I can pick myself out and being part of the group is a good thing because you don't feel so alone. There is camaraderie, being more than one. You get support and everyone in the group is a part of it." One male client became so engrossed in designing this project he ignored this writer when asked to stop working. He didn't want to stop and seemed to be in an artistic trance.

MURAL OF HOPE

Materials: Mural paper, oil pastels, markers, and crayons.

Procedure: Suggest clients work together to create a mural that represents hope. Have them draw images of expectations, wishes, goals, and desires.

Discussion: Explore the symbols presented and their significance. Support clients to maintain a positive attitude while striving to achieve good mental health and recovery from depression and anxiety. Help clients identify realistic goals.

FIGURE 5

Approximately twelve clients of varying ages, challenged with bipolar disorder and schizophrenia, worked together to create this outstanding, colorful mural of hope. Each client designed one or more houses, trees, and various other buildings. They took turns gluing the houses and so on on the paper and then worked together to design the background. There was much problem solving, communication, and creativity involved in this project. Clients took pride in the work and titled it "Dream Community." They admired the design of the mural as well as each others' dwellings. Participants discussed ways in which the houses were self-representative. For instance, one young woman shared that her house was small, warm, and cosy. She explained that she didn't need a lot of things; she just needed love.

During the discussion group members shared that they wished there was a community where everyone could live in harmony regardless of finances, race, culture and so on. "It would be a place where everyone had the same amount of money, lots of food, and were very friendly. People wouldn't care if you had psychological problems because they didn't judge you." Creating this mural elicited a lot of cooperation and smiles among group members.

"SPLASH OF HAPPINESS"

Materials: Mural paper, markers, watercolors, and brushes.

Procedure: Ask clients to draw or paint symbols associated with the theme "Splash of happiness." Suggest they paint (if they are comfortable doing so) splashes of joy on the paper.

Discussion: Discussion focuses on the images, colors, and shapes. Goals include focusing on positive aspects of one's life.

ROAD TO RECOVERY

Materials: Mural paper, markers, oil pastels, magazines, scissors, and glue.

Procedure: A client or the group leader outlines a large road that fills most of the paper. Participants are asked to add people, places, and things that are important for recovery to the road. Everyone has a turn to add drawings and/or photos such as smiling people, men and women exercising, healthy foods, a photo of a doctor and a patient, a dog or cat and so on. The pictures may be drawn or cut out from magazines.

Discussion: Clients share significant items on the road and the way in which they are helpful. Goals include connecting with peers and identifying needs, progress and goals for recovery.

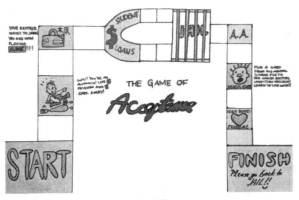

FIGURE 6

A likeable 25-year-old man named Charles, challenged with extreme anxiety and overcoming drug addiction, created "The Game of Acceptance." The game begins with the light pink "Start" square and the player begins traveling down the acceptance road. The first significant square includes a picture of a surprised baby with the words, "Oops! You're an alcoholic! Loss $ Friends and $ Cars—Sorry." The next square consists of a suitcase and the words "Your brother moves to Japan/ You are now playing alone!!!" The road then leads to a horseshoe type of design that focuses on "student loans and jail." The word jail is written within a jail cell and connected to the "student loans" and the green dollar sign. This leads to the AA box, which leads to a picture of a surprised face and the words "mental illness" written under it. Adjoining the drawing of the face Charles wrote, "Pick a card from the mental illness pile to see which exciting conditions you must learn to live with." The next picture box has a heart and "high blood pressure" written in it. Last is the finish square, opposite the start square, which says "Please go back to jail."

Charles shared that he knows he has to accept his situation and move on, especially if he doesn't want to go back to jail! The game is a little tongue in cheek because of Charles' sarcasm, wit, sketches, and smiley face under the exclamation marks next to the word jail. Charles was able to retain a sense of humor, which was an important part of his recovery. He stated he was trying to get to the group each day and get along better with his parents but it was quite a challenge for him. He smiled as other group members complimented his game and supported him as they related to his experiences.

TRAFFIC LIGHT

Materials: Drawing paper, markers, oil pastels, and crayons.

Procedure: Provide the outline of a typical traffic light (a vertical rectangle with three circles which will be colored red, yellow, and green) or have clients draw their own. Direct group members to fill in the first circle red, the second yellow, and the third green. Next ask them to write or illustrate:

- a goal/s next to the green circle

- methods used to try to obtain the goal/s next to the yellow circle

- obstacles to achieving their goal/s next to the red circle.

Discussion: Examine each client's aspirations and barriers to achieving them. Goals include problem solving and exploration of coping skills.

CIRCLE OF STRENGTHS

Materials: Poster board, large circle (you may use the lid of a round garbage can as a template), drawing paper, pencils, markers, magazine photos, glue, and scissors.

Procedure: Divide the circle into as many segments as there are group members. Each participant writes his name in his particular segment. Give clients about 15–20 minutes to find magazine photos that represent strengths and/or have them sketch strengths on drawing paper. Suggest they find photos and/or create drawings sized to fit into the circle segment. They will cut out the photos, and to make the process quicker, they may also cut out their sketches if desired. Next clients take turns gluing the photos or sketches onto one segment of the circle. When everyone has had a turn and all the segments are filled clients discuss their contributions to the circle of strengths.

Discussion: Group members discuss how they relate to the positive characteristics illustrated. They discuss the benefits of interacting with a diverse group of people that have so much to offer. Clients are encouraged to support each other and acknowledge their strengths and those of others.

CELEBRATION MANDALAS

Materials: Paper plates, drawing paper, markers, pencils, magazine photos, construction paper, collage materials, scissors, glue, oil pastels, and crayons.

Procedure: Suggest that clients draw a celebration of their life. Have them include positive symbols related to various stages of their life. These symbols may include people/pets, awards and achievements such as graduations, births, marriages, winning trophies for specific sports such as bowling, learning to drive or swim, winning a contest, being praised for good work, promotions, volunteering, friendships, etc.

Discussion: Explore positive events and the special experiences participants have had during their lifetime. Encourage acknowledgment of the uniqueness of each individual and his exceptional characteristics, achievements, and attributes. Emphasize acknowledgment and expression of gratitude for what he has and what he *can do* as opposed to what he doesn't have and hasn't yet achieved.

FISH IN THE SEA[4]

Materials: Large sheet of mural paper, markers, drawing paper, oil pastels, scissors, glue, paints, markers, brushes, and pencils.

Procedure: Each client creates his own unique fish (between one and three tropical fish). If need be, an outline of various fish may be distributed and colored in by group members. Participants are asked to try to represent a personal characteristic as they design the fish. For example a brightly colored fish might represent a bubbly personality. Next clients cut out their fish and glue it somewhere on the mural paper. Finally, one elected group member or everyone works to create a background.

Discussion: Clients explore the placement of their fish in relation to the others (e.g. is their fish towards the edge of the paper, in the corner, or in the middle of the mural?) As per Tracylynn Navarro, "Each fish reflects unique qualities, as well as a common bond with the other fish in the mural. In a parallel sense, the mural represents the group members individually, as well as the group as a cohesive whole."[5]

SCULPTURE

Materials: Model Magic clay or any other self-hardening clay, and simple plastic sculpture tools.

Procedure: Participants are asked to create a sculpture representing a positive aspect of their personality. The sculpture may be abstract or realistic and the characteristic could be anything decided upon by the artist. Examples may include strength, wisdom, perseverance, being a helper, and good sense of humor.

Discussion: Explore the skill, strength or special characteristic represented. Discuss ways in which the trait helps the client in his daily life and how he can expand upon the trait while continuing to develop additional strengths and skills.

SUCCESS MURAL

Materials: Large sheet of white paper, markers, crayons, oil pastels, and masking tape.

Procedure: Ask group members to take turns drawing one or more of their accomplishments on the paper. Ask them to write the year the achievement took place.

Discussion: Discussion focuses on each group member's accomplishment and the positive feelings it elicited at the time. The meaning of success is explored. Strengths and self-esteem are examined.

FIGURE COLLAGE

Materials: Template of a person, black markers, scissors, drawing paper, glue, magazines, pencils, poster board, crayons, and oil pastels.

Procedure: The group leader draws the outline of a person (12–18 inches (30 × 45 cm) long) on poster board or a thin cardboard and uses it as a template (about three or four templates should be drawn, depending on the size of the group). Each client is given a cardboard template and the therapist encourages the clients to copy the shape of the cardboard figure onto drawing paper. They are then asked to cut out the figure and to use magazine photos, markers, crayons, and so on to fill the in the figure with images, shapes, colors, and designs that reflect positive qualities.

Discussion: Discussion focuses on the client's strengths, hobbies, interests, and achievements. Inner beauty and goodness are explored.

HOPE

Materials: Drawing paper, markers, oil pastels, crayons, glue, scissors, and magazine photos.

Procedure: Discuss the importance of hope and faith in the healing process. Encourage participants to represent the concept of hope through drawing and/or collage work. Support group members to use color, shape, images, and design as well as words to represent their perception of hope and what it means to them.

Discussion: Explore how faith and optimism positively affect emotion, mood, attitude, and behavior. Examine the significance of using one's energy towards overcoming obstacles instead of staying miserable, stuck, and in the victim role. Discuss ways in which one's faith can heal and provide solace in times of adversity.

SIGNATURE STRENGTH

Materials: Drawing paper, markers, pens and pencils, oil pastels and crayons, magazine photos, glue, and scissors.

Procedure: Instruct participants to represent their signature strength (the strength they admire most about themselves) through drawing and/or collage.

Discussion: Explore the positive trait and ask the question, "How can you use this strength more often in your life?" Ask clients to think about the significance of the attribute and ways in which it makes them special.

HEALING

Materials: Magazine photos, drawing paper, markers, oil pastels, glue, scissors, and crayons.

Procedure: Ask group members to think about the following question, "What do you need in order to heal?" Instruct clients to find photos and/or draw pictures of people, places, and things in their life they need to feel better physically and psychologically. Examples may include a partner, a new home, a better attitude, friends, medicine, hope, and love.

Discussion: Explore methods to raise self-worth and hope for the future. Examine ways to self-soothe and heal ourselves. Discuss possible reasons for procrastination and staying stuck in a rut, and emphasize that each individual has the power to begin his own healing process.

SELF-ESTEEM EXERCISE

Materials: Drawing paper, markers, oil pastels, crayon, scissors, and a bucket.

Procedure: Suggest that group members draw their representation of low self-esteem. Encourage them to think of the size, shape, and color of it. Next ask them to cut the representation out. A bucket is placed in the middle of the room and each participant has the choice to keep or throw out his "low self-esteem." Before he throws it out he is supported to say something positive about himself or his life.

Discussion: Participants have the opportunity to gain control of their low self-worth by drawing it and assessing what to do with their representation. Participation in this exercise helps create an awareness of negative attitudes and behavioral patterns. "Why would an individual hold on to his low self-esteem? Where did it come from and how long has he had it?" Encourage exploration of positive self-talk and the importance of taking responsibility for one's attitudes and life direction.

INNER STRENGTH MANDALA

Materials: Paper plate, markers, oil pastels, and crayons.

Procedure: Direct participants to draw their inner strength. Encourage them to think about size, shape, color, and force. Suggest they may add words and images.

Discussion: Explore:

1. What are your reactions to your drawing?

2. Does it reflect your inner strength?

3. What do the size, colors and shapes represent?

4. Has your inner strength always been the same throughout the years?

5. When did you feel the strongest?

6. What gives you strength?

7. What depletes it?

8. Do you have the amount of strength you would ideally like to have?

9. How did you feel while you were drawing? Was the exercise easy, moderate or difficult?

10. If you could change the drawing (your degree of strength) would you?

Write and describe:

1. Write to your mandala (thoughts, feelings about it).

2. Write a few words that describe your mandala (inner strength).

3. Describe the movement of the artwork (does it seem lively, calm, stiff, etc.?).

4. Title the mandala.

BALANCE I

Materials: Copies of a large circle with a line drawn vertically down its center, markers, pencils, pens, colored pencils, oil pastels, and crayons.

Procedure: Distribute copies of the circle. Provide the circle with the word "Stress" typed in the center or have clients write it. Suggest that participants draw and/or list things that create stress in their life on one side of the circle and stress-reducing techniques on the other.

Discussion: Examine the stressors presented and explore methods to reduce them. Share techniques to lessen anxiety and discuss how transforming negative thinking into positive thinking can turn negative experiences into more positive ones. Examine how clients can become more resourceful and learn to view a variety of experiences in a more optimistic and constructive manner. Discuss the importance of balance in one's life and examine methods to create a balanced life style.

DRAGONFLY MANDALA[5]

Materials: Drawing paper, markers, oil pastels, crayons and colored pencils.

Procedure: Clients are introduced to the symbolism of the dragonfly:

"Dragonflies look to be very fragile, but they have 20 times the power in each of their wing strokes when compared to other insects. They have the ability to move in all six directions and can fly up to 45 miles per hour. Their eyes are impressive as they can see 360 degrees around themselves. Dragonflies live most of their lives in the nymph stage and only fly for a few months in their adult stage. Their short life reminds us to live in the moment and live life to its fullest with what we have."

Next instruct participants to create a dragonfly in any way they please, keeping in mind the idea of strength, self-awareness, and mindfulness.

Discussion: Discuss how the life span of the dragonfly can be a lesson in being mindful and the importance of focusing on our strengths and what is in our control. "Let us all remember the small but mighty dragonfly who teaches us to grow with the change in our lives and to live life to the fullest, no matter what is thrown our way."

FIGURE 7

Naomi, a client in her 20s, challenged with bipolar disorder, created this mandala of "A mother dragonfly and her babies." Naomi shared that "the dragonflies are having fun, flying and looking for food. They are a close family and love each other. The mother is looking out for her children. They are free to fly wherever they want without anyone bothering them." Naomi shared that she wished she had a closer relationship with her mother who she described as aloof and selfish. Naomi remarked she would like to have the freedom to fly and do whatever she pleased. She stated she was tired of asking permission to go out with her friends and to drive the car. She shared that she didn't like having to tell her mother where she was going and when she would be home. She liked the description of the dragonfly and agreed that it is important to focus on today because tomorrow hasn't come yet. She said she was going to try to stop worrying about the future and tell her mother that she needs more independence.

MANDALOODLE[6]

Materials: Markers, pen, and ink.

Procedure: Ask clients to create their own mandaloodle after giving the following instructions: The mandaloodle is a mandala/doodle. It is a circle filled with a variety of shapes, lines and figures that connect and blend together to create a personal design. Most of the lines and shapes tend to be small and detailed. The mandaloodle can be created with colors but they are usually black and white. In this way the artist can readily follow the flow of the design. There is no right or wrong way to create a mandaloodle because the idea is to allow your design to evolve by connecting the lines and shapes in any way you choose. If you are not satisfied with one shape another may overlap or be joined in such a way as to change the original form into something else. The mandaloodle represents change and the flow of life. It demonstrates how we can continue to form new ideas and increase creativity in our life. We can make lemonade out of lemons and transform/reinvent ourselves as our circumstances change. The focus of the mandaloodle is to be in the moment, to be mindful and let "our thoughts roll."

Discussion: Explore the unique symbols, shapes, and designs. Encourage participants to share how they felt creating the mandaloodle and the way it reflects their personality, mood, and experiences.

FIGURE 8

A 28-year-old woman challenged with bipolar disorder named Caitlin, designed this mandaloodle. She remarked she enjoyed creating it because she "didn't have to think." She was pleased with the outcome but chose to fill in a small part of it with color because she felt her life was dull and bleak. She had been experiencing severe depression and very low energy. The small triangular filled in area on the right reminded her of a rainbow that was beginning to grow. The snake-like figure represented her friends whom she had to stop associating with because of their drug use and bad influence. Caitlin shared that she liked that she couldn't "mess up" while engaging in this exercise. She enjoyed creating tiny designs and connecting them; she found it relaxing and fun.

NOTES

1. Coined by a Princeton House Client many years ago.
2. Mod Podge is a glue that can also be used like a varnish to protect artwork. Pre-made papier-mâché masks may be purchased through Nasco Arts and Crafts, or clients may create a mask with balloons and papier-mâché paste. The latter might be too messy for seniors.
3. (STOPP) www.getselfhelp.co.uk/stopp.htm, accessed on 9 October 2014.
4. Based on an idea from Tracylynn Navarro MA, ATR-BC.
5. Wendy Hawkins, http://moonlightmandalas.com/, accessed on 9 October 2014.
6. www.mandaloodle.com, accessed on 9 October 2014.

CHAPTER 2

Cognitive Behavioral Therapy

Cognitive behavioral therapy (CBT) focuses on the relationship between thoughts, emotions and behaviors and how each influences the other: "Individuals learn that they can better control their anxiety through self-awareness and monitoring their thoughts."[1] This brief summary just touches upon the therapy developed by Aaron T. Beck during the 1960s. A variety of the techniques presented in this chapter are CBT based, meaning they are related to CBT but not necessarily "pure" CBT.

Clients learn that their thoughts yield emotions, which give rise to specific behaviors. They find out that by changing their thoughts, anxiety and stress can be reduced and self-esteem can be increased. Individuals examine and work to change negative thinking patterns that lower motivation and self-worth. They practice how to transform negative thinking into more positive thinking and reframe displeasing situations so that they are more manageable.

The first step involved in raising self-esteem is self-awareness: becoming aware of destructive thinking and then learning techniques to lessen or eliminate it. "Cognitive behavioral therapy is based on the idea that our thoughts cause our feelings and behaviors, not external things, like people, situations and events."[2] The idea is to change one's reaction to situations and life events, even if the situation or event can't be changed. This type of thinking empowers individuals, giving them increased control over their life and everyday interactions with others.

CBT can be used to treat many disorders including phobias, depression, anxiety, chronic pain, post-traumatic stress disorder, mood swings, eating disorders, and anger management. It helps individuals feel better about themselves as they learn how to cope with daily stressors and responsibilities "The goal of cognitive behavioral therapy is to help people learn to recognize negative patterns of thought, evaluate their validity, and replace them with healthier ways of thinking."[3] CBT focuses on specific problems; it is goal oriented and educational. The therapy has a here and now focus. The therapy is time limited and clients are expected to take an active role in their own therapy. The therapist assists the client and helps facilitate the process of change.

As Nemade, Staats Reiss, and Dombeck state, "Depression takes place because people develop a disposition to view situations and circumstances in habitually negative and biased ways, leading them to habitually experience negative feelings and emotions as a result" and "Core beliefs serve as a filter through which people see the world."[4] They are strongly held beliefs that people hold onto for many years, often from childhood onwards. When the core beliefs are positive self-esteem is raised but when they are negative self-esteem diminishes. "Core beliefs influence the development of 'intermediate beliefs', which are related attitudes, rules and assumptions that follow from core beliefs."[4] During therapy individuals learn to identify and then change negative and irrational core beliefs. They do this by questioning them and looking for evidence for and against them. Some questions include:

1. Is there any evidence for this belief?

2. What is the evidence against this belief?

3. What is the worst that can happen if you give up this belief?

4. What is the best that can happen?

During CBT therapy clients decide which goals they would like to pursue and the therapist helps the client achieve them through teaching, listening, and support. Homework is an essential part of the therapy and is usually given on a regular basis. The techniques need to be practiced frequently. This way the individual will learn how to integrate the skills so that they become routine: an integral part of daily life. Clients learn specific skills such as identifying distorted thinking patterns, examining core beliefs and finding evidence to prove or disprove their negative beliefs and erroneous thoughts. Clients learn that they can change the way they perceive situations and therefore help to change unsettling feelings and resulting behaviors. Clients use affirmations, positive self-talk, and self-awareness to improve their attitudes and reactions to events, experiences, and people they encounter.

Finding new coping strategies leads to lasting changing and improved behavior and self-esteem. Clients realize they can control their thoughts instead of having their thoughts control them. Clients learn to solve problems that have been long standing.

Art therapy enhances much of the CBT process by providing individuals with the opportunity to creatively express core beliefs as well as healthy and distorted thinking patterns. This helps create greater self-awareness since clients are easily able to clarify and share emotions through color, line, collage, design, image, and shape. Art creates a clear and less threatening means to identify and process emotions and patterns of thinking and behavior. It serves as a steadfast canvas to observe, analyze and refer to as needed.

PAST/PRESENT

Materials: Drawing paper, markers, pastels, and colored pencils.

Procedure: Clients fold their paper in half. On one side of the paper they draw something about themselves from the past and on the other side of the paper they illustrate something they know about themselves at the moment. It can be a personality characteristic, something they own, a person in their life and so on. It can be represented realistically or abstractly.

Discussion: Goals include self-awareness and exploration of personality characteristics and environment. Clients share ways in which the past has affected their attitude, personality, and behavior in the present.

COGNITIVE DISTORTIONS

Materials: Sheet of distortions (see below), pens, pencils, markers, drawing paper, and lined writing paper.

Example of a few cognitive distortions:

1. **Black and white thinking**—viewing the world in absolutes. It is only one way or the other way. For example, it is a good day; it is a bad day. There is no gray area.

2. **Overgeneralization**—the individual sees one unfortunate event as a neverending series of negative events. For example, Jon fails one math test and decides he will never pass another math test again.

3. **Mental filter**—choosing one negative aspect about a person, situation or experience and focusing solely on the problem—not acknowledging any positive aspects related to what is occurring. For example, you are on a picnic; it's a sunny, beautiful day and after a while you notice a family of ants on the picnic table. You then declare "The day is ruined; we have ants."

4. **Discounting the positive**—rejecting the positives by finding a reason that they are not valid. For example, Jack compliments Mary on her blouse and Mary says "Oh, this is so old; all my clothes are hand-me-downs."

5. **Magnification**—exaggerating problems and negative experiences. For example, you have a doctor appointment and worry that he will find a tumor and you will be immediately hospitalized.

6. **Labeling**—categorizing yourself and/or others in one specific way—no gray area allowed. For example, if you fail one test you label yourself a loser.

7. **Should statements**—placing a judgment on yourself and others, which usually increases stress and decreases self-esteem. It is an irrational way of thinking in that you judge what you must be doing or how you must be acting. For example, "I should be married by age 30," or "I should have a good job by age 35"; "I should lose five pounds." It often sets you up for failure and guilt.

8. **Blaming**—taking responsibility for an event that isn't in your control or that has nothing to do with you. For example, a group member leaves the room and you automatically assume you said something to hurt his feelings.

Procedure: Participants receive a list of cognitive distortions, which they read and discuss together. Next clients are asked to choose one distortion they have engaged in, in the past, or continue to experience on a regular basis. Ask them to write about their experiences and then suggest they illustrate the way they felt. They may create an abstraction using color, shape, and form, or a more realistic image, figure, or scene.

Discussion: Explore reasons for utilizing distortions and the toll that erroneous thinking takes on our self-esteem, attitude, behavior, and relationships. Examine healthier methods of thinking and behaving. Support the sharing of more positive and realistic ways to view problems and concerns.

Bill, a 39-year-old client, shared that he uses "all or nothing" thinking. He said he was tired of "holding everything in and bottling everything up." He remarked that he wanted to fight, to punch someone in the face. Bill believed this would relieve him of his stress, anxiety and inner turmoil. He said he wanted to drink, brawl and gamble—especially gamble. He announced he wanted to gamble until he either lost everything or won enough so that he had no more financial problems. He remarked that he didn't care about struggling any more. He wanted "it all or nothing."

A lot of the session was spent encouraging him to try to fight his impulses and not to allow himself to become a victim of his distorted outlook on life. He said he hated his job and his co-workers, and his "so called friends were threatening him." A peer suggested he change jobs and move. This seemed quite threatening, but Bill appeared pensive for a few seconds and admitted it was something he never contemplated before, Towards the end of the session Bill's demeanor, though still very stressed, changed from furious to more relaxed. He seemed a little less determined to follow the harmful and self-destructive path previously described.

Bill was able to depict his feelings while thinking in a "black and white manner."

FIGURE 9

Bill decided to create an abstract view of his present thought process. He shared that the glasses represent seeing things clearly and having his life run smoothly (his wish). He emphasizes this point with the statement on the bottom of the page, "Best Life Now." The person who looks like she's engaged in an acrobatic dive represents his need to "dive right into life." This symbolizes his all or nothing thinking; he doesn't consider the consequences of his actions. Bill stated he noticed that his eyes (the glasses) were situated far from his "ideal life" because he sees possible success and contentment far into the future. The colorful rectangular shapes represent the obstacles standing in the way of his happiness. When asked, Bill remarked some of the obstacles include his rage, stubbornness, need for excitement, and occasional paranoia. He shared that it is very difficult for him to control his anger and he is trying to work on this issue in therapy.

FIGURE 10

Gloria, a 59-year-old woman challenged with bipolar disorder, drew this creature she titled "Ursula." She related the figure to the Ursula character from "The Little Mermaid." Ursula related to the distorted thinking patterns of blame and magnification according to Gloria. She described the figure in detail: "Ursula is my friend Theresa; she is like an octopus in that she wants to control everything and everyone. She wants to take whatever I have and keep it for herself. She engulfs everyone that comes in contact with her and she is evil. She has a bright red, evil smile, but that is a facade because when she gets you in her clutches she will eat you alive. She lures you in by smiling and acting like you are important; she will even do you a favor or two. That is just in the beginning to make you feel comfortable, but then she attacks and you are in her clutches and it is very difficult to get out of them."

Gloria related to the theme of blame because she acknowledged that she tends to blame her friend Theresa (Ursula) for all her misfortunes. Sometimes Theresa has something to do with her problems but Gloria did share that she uses Theresa (Ursula) as a scapegoat and makes her friend seem more sinister than she really is. It seems that it helps Gloria cope with her own problems when she blames Theresa for being the main source of her woes. For example, Gloria's husband left her because he felt she was too needy, too depressed, and boring. Gloria believed or wanted to believe Theresa was to blame because she used to interfere in their life all the time and was often rude to her husband.

Gloria shared that she will try to be more realistic and take more responsibility for what occurs in her life. She acknowledged that it would be healthier to use her energy to solve her problems rather than put blame on others.

NOURISHING AND DEPLETING ACTIVITIES I

Materials: Drawing paper, glue, scissors, magazine photos, markers, and oil pastels.

Procedure: Participants fold their paper in half. On one side of the paper they draw nourishing activities and on the other side they draw depleting activities. Magazine photos may be added if desired.

Examples of nourishing activities:

1. exercising
2. drawing
3. reading
4. journaling
5. cooking
6. yoga
7. gardening
8. meditating
9. dancing
10. bicycle riding.

Examples of depleting activities:

1. driving long distances when there is a lot of traffic
2. cleaning the house (if you don't enjoy cleaning)
3. preparing to move (packing belongings)
4. doing tedious chores and errands
5. waiting in long lines in stores
6. studying a difficult subject
7. getting a divorce
8. working very long hours
9. playing a game or sport and feeling pressured to win
10. doing favors for friends (when you are very tired and don't really want to help).

Discussion: We need to become aware of depleting routines and activities. Once we are cognizant of the positives and negatives of our life style, we can work on methods to lessen stress, depression, and frustration. We can explore methods to make unpleasant experiences more bearable.

Explore the nourishing and depleting activities depicted in the artwork. Discuss which activities are absolutely necessary and which ones can be eliminated from our daily routine. Examine methods to transform the depleting experiences into more nourishing ones. For example, listening to music in the car makes a long drive less tedious and reading a magazine will make standing in long lines less boring. Suggest that clients share a time they took a depleting activity and transformed it into a nourishing activity. Questions such as: "How did it feel to change the activity and how did the change in activity affect your mood?" might be discussed.

NOURISHING AND DEPLETING ACTIVITIES II

Materials: Writing paper, pencils, and pens.

Procedure: Ask clients to create two separate lists. On the first list suggest they write all the activities they engage in during the working week and on the second list include all the activities they engage in at the weekend. Next have them place an N (for nourishing) next to the nourishing activities and a D (for depleting) next to the depleting activities. Suggest they list all the activities they can think of including: waking up, getting showered, brushing teeth, eating breakfast, etc.

Discussion: Questions for self-awareness:

1. How many Ns (nourishing) and how many Ds (depleting) activities did you check off the working week? How many for the weekend?

2. Which activities would you like to add to enrich your life and sense of well-being?

3. Which activities would you like to change?

4. What types of healthy, nourishing activities did you engage in when you were younger? Would you consider engaging in them now?

5. How can you lead a more balanced life style? Why is that important?

6. Is there a more positive way to view some of the depleting activities that must be done?

7. Can you think of activities that are presently depleting but were nourishing in the past?

8. How does self-talk play a role in nourishing and depleting activities?

9. When was the last time you engaged in a nourishing activity? How did you feel?

10. Share one nourishing activity you engaged in today. How did it make you feel?

CORE BELIEF MANDALA

Core beliefs are strongly held beliefs, often possessed since childhood. They are the essence of how we see ourselves and the world. They are difficult to change and often contribute to low self-esteem. Unhealthy beliefs will often distort our view of the world and lead to distorted thoughts.

Materials: Paper plates, drawing paper, markers, magazines, glue, scissors, markers, and colored pencils.

Procedure: Participants use the plate to trace a circle in the middle of the paper. They fill in the circle with drawings, words, sketches, and magazine photos that reflect their core beliefs. On the outer rim of the circle they use words, phrases, illustrations, etc.

to demonstrate evidence that the negative core beliefs are not an accurate reflection of who they are today.

Discussion: Explore how negative core beliefs can have a harmful impact on all aspects of our lives and self-esteem. These beliefs can keep individuals prisoners of their erroneous thoughts, stopping them from learning, growing, and having healthy relationships. When people are made aware of these beliefs they can better understand how they began, what triggered and triggers them, and how they affect unhealthy patterns of behavior. They can then begin to work towards lessening or eliminating them, especially when using evidence that allows them to see that they are valuable and worthy of respect.

Claire was an attractive woman in her early 70s who was challenged with a deep depression. She drew a circle filled with negative words and phrases, and she also added magazine photos, which included a sad-looking dog, a sick child, a tired-looking man, and a woman who clearly had migraine. Some of the words she added were: "stupid, nothing, can't do it, lonely, can't think, hopeless, overwhelmed, and confused." She remarked she believed her mandala was reflective of her personality.

Claire had great difficulty finding evidence to dispute these claims. On the outer rim of the circle she placed a series of question marks. Group members were very supportive of her. They suggested that she wasn't seeing herself the way they saw her. One woman asked her if she would include the words "sweet, kind, and thoughtful" on the outer rim of the circle. Another client asked her to add that she was helpful and always willing to go out of her way for others. Reluctantly, Claire added these affirmations to her circle, but her hand was shaky as she was writing. She will need to continue to examine the evidence that she is most valuable and likable. It may take quite a long time, because change is very difficult and the negative beliefs have been ingrained for many years.

CORE BELIEFS

Core beliefs are strongly held beliefs towards oneself and others. They are often deeply ingrained in us and frequently "owned" since childhood. They may be positive and/or negative, and they affect our attitude, behavior, mood, thoughts, and self-esteem.

Self-awareness is the first step towards working through negative core beliefs. In order to change them one has to first become aware that they exist. Acknowledging and accepting the beliefs is a major hurdle. Next exploring ways to change and/or transform them into more realistic thoughts gives the individual freedom to think more positively and boosts their self-esteem. They are often able to be more assertive and lead more productive and meaningful lives.

Materials: Drawing paper, pens, pencils, markers, glue, scissors, and magazine photos.

Procedure: Instruct participants to fold their paper in half. On one half of the paper ask them to write, draw, and/or glue photos of positive core beliefs and on the other side have them add negative core beliefs. Suggest they may draw, sketch, or use photos from magazines. They may want to utilize colors, shapes, and forms to express their thoughts. Lastly ask participants to describe how and when their core beliefs emerged (e.g. friends, family, experiences, their environment, teachers, etc.).

Discussion: Explore the various beliefs and their effect on daily life and self-esteem. Examine whether the positive side is stronger than the negative side and ways in which the negative side can be transformed. Explore whether or not the negative core beliefs are valid now. Begin to examine the evidence to support or dismiss these beliefs as accurate. Share ways to focus on strengths as opposed to weaknesses.

Frank, a lanky man in his 60s, working through a major depression, emphasized his negative traits. He drew a picture of a small man standing next to a very large man with a long gray beard.

He remarked that his father always berated him for everything he did and "slapped him around" for any minor disturbance. His father always seemed angry and never praised him. He shared that he still feels tiny next to his 90-year-old father who is now hunched over and walks with a cane: "Some of his strength is gone, but he is still freaking nasty." Frank blamed his father's bullying on his lack of confidence and unwillingness to take risks in life. "He made me feel like dirt a kid and that's how I feel now."

Frank was able to draw a small rainbow on the positive side of the page. It represented a woman he had recently met who seemed to like him. He mentioned that she was assertive and had approached him at a party. He said he was quite surprised because he would never have approached such an attractive woman. Frank was able to see that maybe there was some hope for him, "At least someone seems to like me." He was also able to understand that his father's attitude toward him gave birth to his negative belief system, and that he had the ability to begin to change his thoughts if he chose to do so.

THOUGHTS, EMOTIONS, BEHAVIOR

Materials: Drawing paper, markers, oil pastels, scissors, and glue.

Procedure: Participants are given two sheets of paper. The first sheet is divided into three parts. In the first section clients illustrate a thought. In the second section they draw an emotion and in the third section they draw a behavior. Next clients cut out the three sections and then re-paste them on another sheet of paper in the order in which they believe they belong.

Discussion: Encourage participants to share the order of their artwork. Explore how thoughts yield emotions, which yield behavior and *vice-versa*. Examine how thought, behavior, and emotion interrelate and how they actually can be perceived in terms of a circle (no beginning or ending); each thought/feeling/emotion affects the other. Share how each word impacts attitude and self-esteem, and how they are all influenced by one's environment and past and present experiences.

Thought: The capacity or faculty of thinking, reasoning, imagining, etc.

A consideration or reflection.[5]

Thinking: To have a conscious mind, to some extent of reasoning, remembering experiences, making rational decisions, etc.

Emotion: A conscious mental reaction (as anger or fear) subjectively experienced as strong feeling usually directed toward a specific object and typically accompanied by physiological and behavioral changes in the body.[6]

Behavior: Anything that an organism does involving action and response to stimulation

The response of an individual, group, or species to its environment.[7]

SELF-ESTEEM INVENTORY

Materials: Pens, pencils, and lined paper.

Procedure: Everyone receives a sheet of lined writing paper. Have clients divide their paper in half and write "strengths" on one side of the paper and "weaknesses" on the other. Suggest participants write down as many strengths and weaknesses as they can think of, and then ask them to add a description of a time they acted in a way that demonstrated positive or negative traits, actions, or abilities.

Discussion: Participants review their inventory and add up their positives and negatives, and share which is dominant. Next clients review methods to transform their weaknesses to strengths, and revisit any negative thinking. They are supported to focus on achievements, assets, and strengths.

In many instances clients are not aware of their strengths until they experience this exercise. Self-esteem and self-awareness are enhanced and participants have the opportunity to focus on what they can do instead of what they can't do.

Bob, a divorced man in his early 60s was trying to overcome clinical depression. He felt defeated in life. He lived with his children and rarely left their home. He said he hated the fact that he couldn't afford his own apartment. He was lonely, bored, frustrated, fearful and he had a completely defeatist attitude. He was not able to share any positive abilities or traits before taking part in this exercise. He refused to join groups or volunteer out of fear of the unknown and fear of being rejected by others. He doubted his abilities although he was previously an accountant in New York City. After examining his positive and negative traits he realized that even though he "used up all his money" on his three daughters over the years he indeed raised three successful, good-hearted, happy human beings. He admitted that he was a good father. He also realized that he had been successful in his work and at one point in his life he had friends and an extended family. He almost smiled when group members told him he was noble for putting his family's needs before his own. With support from peers he acknowledged that he had mathematical capability and he had the ability to reach out to others if he "chose to do it." He did say that he was shocked to see so many positives written down.

Bob went to many different types of therapy groups and was in the outpatient program for a few months, but eventually he began volunteering, taking tiny steps forward, and working towards socializing and opening himself up to new life possibilities.

EVIDENCE I

We often behave in unconstructive ways, have negative attitudes, or view ourselves disdainfully because of unhealthy core beliefs. In order to begin changing negative core beliefs we look at the evidence that is used as a basis for the belief. When current evidence disproves our negative beliefs we can then examine our thinking, and become cognizant that our thinking may be distorted and unrealistic. Once this takes place change is possible.

Materials: Pen, pencil, and handouts.

Procedure: Copy and hand out the following scenarios and explore the negative core beliefs and distorted thinking that clouds the individuals' judgment in the various situations. Group members may circle problems in communication and thought processes in each situation.

Scenarios: looking for evidence and distorted thinking

Is Jack worthy or unworthy? Look for evidence to support your belief.

Jack is 40 years old and is in the middle of a rather harsh divorce. He has been married for 20 years and he has two pre-teen children. His wife decided he doesn't work hard enough to support the family. She is tired of her full-time position as a school aid and wants to work part time so she can be home for the children and also have time to do housework. She would like to own her own home and is fed up with their small two-bedroom apartment. Jack works nine-hour days in a home goods store loading and unloading large pieces of wood and stone used for home repairs. His salary is a little above minimum wage. He tries to help his children with their schoolwork but sometimes he is so tired after dinner he can't focus and needs to relax and watch television. Jack feels like a failure. He says he is worthless.

Is Marie intelligent or unintelligent? What is the evidence to support your belief?

Marie has struggled with science her whole life. She just can't grasp the concepts. She fears she may fail chemistry this semester. She stresses while doing her homework every night.

She is excelling in Spanish class and she is extremely creative. Her artwork is unique and hanging in the principal's office. Her parents told her if she doesn't pass chemistry she will not be allowed to go on vacation with her friend's family this summer. They are going to Spain. Marie complains to her friend Denise that she is "So stupid. I don't understand anything."

Is Max brave or a coward? What is the evidence to support your belief?

Max and his friend Bryan were walking down the street in Manhattan. They were having a great time browsing and snacking. Max received a phone call on his cell phone and attempted to take it out of his pocket when a young man jumped him, grabbed the phone and ran away. Bryan started running after the man but he ran too fast and got away. Max was really upset. After some time he thought more about the incident and began to feel badly. He told his parents he felt like a failure for not trying to get his cell phone back: "I didn't even run after the man." He told a friend, "Bryan was so brave and I just stood still; I did nothing." In the past whenever someone teased his friend Glenn, he would stand up for Glenn and tell the other young men to leave Glenn alone. One time a bully punched him for doing this but he ignored him and walked away.

Discussion: Encourage group members to examine how their own distortions color their judgment at times. Explore the following questions to better understand why someone may be experiencing low self-esteem and holding on to their negative core beliefs:

1. Did I lose something recently such as my job and am I basing my self-esteem on that loss?

2. Am I basing my self-esteem on the behavior of someone other than myself such as my partner or child?

3. Am I basing my feelings on how I was treated as a child? For example, perhaps I was teased or mistreated by others.

4. Am I comparing myself to others?

5. Am I self deprecating because of an illness or disability that can't be helped, or a physical trait such as crossed eyes?

6. Am I blaming myself for past mistakes?

7. Do I feel unworthy because I need extra assistance and I am a little more dependent on others than in the past?

8. Am I perhaps feeling unworthy because of illness or other problems such as stress or relationship issues?

INTERNAL BARRIER MANDALA

Internal barriers may include negative thoughts, attitudes, guilt, distorted thinking, and inability to work on change. They might entail holding steadfast to the role of victim and experiencing the inability to put one's life into perspective and see the "big picture." They might include procrastination, poor time management, fear of change, anxiety, and anger.

Materials: Drawing paper, markers, pencils and pens, oil pastels, paint, scissors, glue, and magazine photos.

Procedure: Ask group members to create a mandala of their internal barrier/s. They may include images, words, shapes, colors, and photos that represent what is keeping them from moving forward.

Discussion: In order to accept ourselves and move forward it is helpful to remove the internal barriers that are keeping us from functioning appropriately and being successful and content.

Explore the size, shape, color and images that compose the barrier. Discuss if it would be easy or difficult to break it down and explore how long it has been in existence. Discuss the possible benefits of the barrier and what would happen if it wasn't there. How would life be different? Would there be benefits in quality of life and self-esteem?

PALETTE OF EMOTIONS

Emotions: "A state of feeling; a conscious mental reaction (as anger or fear) subjectively experienced as strong feeling usually directed toward a specific object and typically accompanied by physiological and behavioral changes in the body."[8]

Materials: Palettes (the therapist might draw a palette for each group member), markers, and pencils, colored pencils.

Procedure: Each client is given a palette already outlined on a piece of white paper. The group participants are asked to fill in the circles of the palette (which are normally filled in with paint) with words, designs, colors, and pictures to express a variety of emotions.

Discussion: Expression of thoughts, issues, and feelings are focused upon. It is very important that participants are able to understand and connect with their emotions in order to gain greater self-awareness, which in turn leads to greater self-esteem.

FEELING ASSOCIATIONS

Materials: Drawing paper, markers, crayons, and oil pastels.

Procedure: Suggest that clients draw a quick sketch to represent at least five of the following feelings:

- happiness

- anger

- anxiety
- boredom
- sadness
- fear
- loneliness
- frustration
- depression
- shame
- confusion
- feeling overwhelmed.

Discussion: Examine the drawings in terms of intensity, color, and symbolism. Use the artwork to explore the ways in which clients express or hold in their feelings, and explore how emotions impact behavior and attitude. Goals include identification of feelings and learning healthy methods to share them.

ACCEPTANCE I

Materials: Drawing paper, markers, oil pastels, and crayons.

Procedure: Ask group members to draw things they have accepted in their life, e.g. less stamina, moving to a smaller home, certain health conditions, loss of friends and/or family members, divorce, or never marrying, etc.

Discussion: Clients share their losses (an important move toward reconciliation and healing). They share experiences, both good and bad, and examine how they endured when life was difficult. Goals include exploration of acceptance, change, and examination of methods to attain health, recovery, and future goals.

FIGURE 11

Donna, a 30-year-old woman challenged with bipolar disorder, created "a profile of acceptance." The first part of the profile was designed carefully and in detail. Donna took a lot of time and effort to create an attractive veil of sequins. She spent much time thumbing through magazines until she found just the right eyes, and the design under the eyes took quite some time to complete; the colors were carefully chosen. Donna was very pleased with the woman but stated she could not add more to the portrait. When asked the reason, she shared that she was "a work in progress" and didn't know who she was, what her goals were, or where she was going in life. Donna remarked that she wasn't sure whether she wanted to stay in school or find a job, live at home or on her own, or stay with her boyfriend of six weeks or leave him. She shared that all of these decisions were difficult for her but she had accepted, at least for the time being, that she was in process and would need to continue to learn how to take better care of herself, take her medications as prescribed and try to improve her communication skills so she could get along better with others. She liked a comment shared by a peer who thought the attractiveness of the figure might show there was hope "that she could do better." It is ironic that Donna didn't include the mouth (there is just a faint outline) because she often speaks rapidly and frequently, which tends to keep people at bay. This behavior prevents her from forming meaningful relationships. Donna wanted to give this writer her picture, and she was very pleased when I told her I'd like to take a photo of it. She asked if it was okay that it wasn't complete and she seemed to breathe a sigh of relief when she was told "it was fine."

THOUGHT STOPPING

Materials: Drawing paper, scissors, glue, markers, oil pastels, pens, and pencils.

Procedure: Discuss how thought stopping can help decrease stress and improve the quality of one's life. Clients will be asked to say, "Stop" to themselves, quietly or out loud, and immediately change what they are thinking and their activity in order to effectively stop irrational and/or troubling thoughts.

Ask group members to write out the word "Stop" using large, colorful letters. Next have them cut the word out and place it next to them. Then suggest they draw or write a troubling and/or recurring thought on a sheet of drawing paper. Next ask clients to share their drawings and/or descriptions, and then have them glue the word "Stop" on top of the picture.

Discussion: Discussion focuses on the obsessive thoughts and the way it felt to physically place the word "Stop" on top of them (symbolically gaining control). Goals include identifying uncomfortable feelings/thoughts, gaining mastery over obsessions, and exploring coping skills.

WORRY

Materials: Writing paper, pens, and pencils.

Procedure: Discuss the meaning of the word "worry" with clients. Ask group members their thoughts and then share the following description: *Worry consists of future-oriented, often catastrophic thinking largely consisting of words rather than images. It affects how one behaves, thinks, feels, and relates to others. It can be productive or non productive. Productive worry leads to direct action to solve a problem or reduce a future threat. Un-productive worry paralyzes and inhibits problems solving. People tend to worry about a variety of themes including: finances, health, family, safety, and relationships.*

Now have clients list five things they worry about. Next to the worries ask them to rate the level of stress associated with the worry on a 1–10 scale, where 10 is the most stressful and 1 is the least stressful.

Lastly, ask them to ponder and then share:

- Is your worry productive?

- Is the problem solvable?

- Is the worry motivating you to take action?

- Are you generating potential solutions?

- Are you acting on those solutions?

- What would be the pros and cons of mastering your worry?

- Name one worry that you can begin to control right now.

Discussion: Clients explore realistic and unrealistic fears and how they affect their feelings, mood, behavior, and actions. Goals include identifying concerns and then trying to adapt coping skills to help control worrying.

THOUGHT TRIANGLE

Materials: Drawing paper, markers, oil pastels, pencils, pens, and crayons.

Procedure: Have group members draw a triangle in the middle of the paper or provide a sheet with a triangle already on it. Participants then draw a circle on each edge of the triangle. The top circle will become a head with a face, the bottom circles will become feet. The shapes are now transforming into a figure. Instruct clients to complete the person and then to write the thoughts the person is thinking by his head, the emotions the person is feeling by one foot, and the behavior of the person by the other foot. Encourage the group members to try to find a connection between the thoughts, emotions, and behavior of this fictitious individual.

Discussion: In cognitive behavioral therapy the concept that thoughts yield emotions which yield behavior, and *vice-versa*, can be difficult for some individuals to understand. By creating a drawing such as this, participants can better understand that their thoughts can have a strong impact on their attitudes, mood, and actions. Have participants share the person they drew and reflect on their own experiences with thoughts acting as a catalyst for their emotions and resulting behaviors.

SELF-IMAGE MANDALA

Materials: Drawing paper, paper plates, markers, oil pastels, magazines, scissors, glue, and cut paper.

Procedure: Outline a circle (mandala) using a paper plate. Instruct clients as follows: "Fill in the circle with words and images about yourself that flow through your mind during the course of the day." Ask them to circle the positive images and words.

Discussion: Explore how many positive and how many negative words/images are included. Discuss whether there is a significant discrepancy between the positive and negative words images.

Explore the importance of self-awareness and methods to transform negative thinking into more positive thinking and self talk.

PAST/PRESENT

Materials: Drawing paper, markers, pastels, and colored pencils.

Procedure: Clients fold their paper in half. On one side of the paper they draw something about themselves from the past and on the other side they illustrate something they know about themselves at the moment. It can be a personality characteristic, something they own, a person in their life, etc. It can be represented realistically or abstractly.

Discussion: Goals include self-awareness and exploration of personality characteristics and environment. Clients share ways in which the past has affected their attitude, personality, and behavior in the present.

EVIDENCE II

Materials: Drawing paper, markers, colored pencils, oil pastels, and crayons.

Procedure: Ask clients to illustrate a core belief that has been hurtful to think about. They may utilize lines, shape, design, and color to represent the belief and its intensity. They then describe it and reflect how it has been harmful over the years and examine how the thought has affected behavior, emotions, relationships, psychological state, and attitudes. Next, they list evidence to disprove this belief.

Discussion: Explore how our core beliefs affect all aspects of our life and can keep us from pursuing our dreams and goals. Support group members to question their erroneous thoughts. The questions can include the following:

1. Is there another explanation for why I am feeling this way?

2. What is the effect of my belief/s?

3. How would life be different if I changed my beliefs?

4. What would I tell a friend who had these beliefs?

5. How long have I had this belief?

6. Who or what has played a role in the forming of my core belief?

7. Do I have to hold on to my hurtful beliefs? Can I let go of them? What might happen?

SELF-ESTEEM FLAG

Materials: Drawing paper, markers, oil pastels, and colored pencils.

Procedure: Ask clients to create a personal flag full of images and words that represent their strengths and positive qualities.

Examples of words to describe their personality:

- happy
- positive
- optimistic
- caring
- loving
- smart
- supportive
- creative
- encouraging
- talented
- clean

- gentle
- easy going
- neat
- hopeful
- attractive
- sincere
- good listener
- focused
- non judgmental
- good natured
- outgoing
- peaceful
- persevering
- logical
- gentle
- easy going
- able/positive
- polite
- good mother, father, sister, brother, aunt, uncle, grandmother, grandfather, cook, organizer, co-worker, friend.

Discussion: When people view themselves in a positive manner they are generally more content and successful. They have more fulfilling relationships. Self-acceptance and focusing on positive as opposed to negative traits will help increase self-esteem.

Encourage clients to explore their strengths and positive characteristics. Ask them to share ways they contribute to their families and to society. Suggest that they focus on what is in their control and what they can do as opposed to what is out of their control and what they can't do.

STOP SIGN II

Materials: Drawing paper, markers, oil pastels, crayons, scissors, glue, buttons, pom-poms, and various collage materials.

Procedure: Ask clients to draw an eye-catching stop sign. They can decorate it with markers, paint, sequins, buttons, etc.

Discussion: Explore the acronym STOPP and examine how it helps individuals deal with stress, anger, and anxiety when dealing with tense situations:

S: Stop

T: Take a breath

O: Observe:

> *What am I thinking?*
>
> *What am I reacting to?*
>
> *What am I feeling in my body?*

P: Pull back:

> *Put it into perspective*
>
> *See the bigger picture*
>
> *Is this fact or opinion?*
>
> *How would someone else see this?*

P: Practice what works

> *What's the best thing for me to do in this situation?*
>
> *"Try not to act merely in the moment. Pull back from the situation. Take a wider view; compose yourself."*

BEHAVIORAL ACTIVATION: PROFILE COLLAGE[9-11]

Materials: Template of human profile, pens and pencils, markers, oil pastels, magazines, cut paper, glue, and scissors.

Procedure: Have clients fill in the profile with shapes, images, photos, words, etc. that symbolize work/professional goals, positive activities, and strategies to help create a life that is uplifting and productive.

Discussion: The goal of this exercise is to increase self-awareness and to explore the amount of "meaningful" activity in clients' everyday lives.

"When people feel depressed or anxious, they may be less likely to do the things they enjoy, and therefore, it is important to learn how to be more active. Behavioral activation is way to do this. The goal is to help people get more active in areas of their life that are pleasurable and enjoyable. Being more connected and involved with these experiences can improve your mood."

"Behavioral activation involves creating a daily schedule filled with meaningful activities that increase mood while becoming aware of avoidance behaviors and activities that lower self-esteem and decrease mood. Behavioral activation usually incorporates activity monitoring, assessment of life goals and values, activity scheduling, skills training, problem solving, effective communication training, and relaxation training. It works to manage avoidance and isolation."

Basics of Behavioral Activation:

"The main goals in behavioral activation are to increase activity levels (and prevent avoidance behaviors) and help the patient take part in positive and rewarding activities which can improve his or her mood."[9]

1. *Behavioral activation attempts to reduce avoidance and*

2. *increase positive reinforcement and routine.*

3. *People are refocused on goals and valued directions in their life.*

Steps involved:

1. Create a list of several short and long term goals that you would like to accomplish. For example, a short term goal might include cleaning your home and a long term goal might include finding a job or having a relationship.

2. Create a list of minor activities that you can complete each week, which will help you to attain your short term and long term goals. For example, if you want to go back to college (long term goal) you might start by reading a book about your chosen field (activity). A short term goal might be to take an online course focusing on your area of interest.

3. On a sheet of paper write down all the activities you want to engage in during the week. Also indicate how many times you want to engage in the activity and for how long. For example, someone who writes that they want to pursue jewelry design as an activity may also write down that they want to create jewelry three times a week for an hour.

4. Each day track your progress. When you have completed a goal for that week, place a check mark next to the activity to indicate its completion.

5. If you complete all your goals for a certain week, reward yourself.

6. Each week build upon the previous week. Carry activities from week to week. If there are certain activities that you want to make into a habit (for example, weekly exercise), repetition is important.

FIGURE 12

A 32-year-old woman named Jessica, who was recovering from clinical depression, included many of her hopes, dreams, and goals in this profile collage. She was able to acknowledge that some of her plans, such as eating in a healthier manner and adopting a dog, could be quickly implemented, but other plans like getting married and having a child would have to wait until she was psychologically ready and found a man who was mature, trustworthy, and dependable. Her last boyfriend was verbally abusive and extremely irresponsible.

Jessica added photos of people engaged in sports such as bicycle riding and skiing; she stated she needed to lose 15 pounds (around 6 kg) and become more active. She shared that she used to go to the gym almost daily but lost all motivation to exercise after breaking up with her boyfriend. Jessica included cartoons of a woman reading and a woman in bed, and stated she used to read all the time but had difficulty focusing for the past few months. She was hoping she would be able to begin reading magazines and short stories in the near future. She stated she knew she had to practice better sleep hygiene and attempt to get at least 6 hours of sleep a night so she could increase her energy and improve her mood.

Jessica viewed her collage as hopeful. She expressed a love of nature, pets, and people. A photo of a woman who appears very stressed is situated at the bottom right corner of the neck. Jessica remarked that she planned to practice meditation, yoga, and other relaxation techniques in order to lessen her anxiety. The part of the collage she liked the best is on the left side of the head. It is a photo of a man kissing a woman; a baby is holding onto his head while sitting on his shoulders. Jessica stated her main goal was to get married and have a child. Jessica seemed pleased with her work; she remarked that she planned to use the profile as a vision board to inspire her to accomplish all of her goals.

CBT BINGO[12]

Materials: Copies of a grid that includes five squares across and five squares down, index cards, colored markers, pens, and pencils.

Procedure:

A. The group leader prepares the master grid

1. In the upper right hand corner of each square of the grid draw a small circle about the size of a large pea.

2. In each square write a question relating to CBT. Examples of questions might include:

    • List two thought distortions.

    • How can labeling lower self-esteem?

    • How do thoughts affect emotions and behaviors?

- What is a core belief? Share one of your core beliefs.

- How can we begin to change negative core beliefs?

- Share one nourishing and one depleting activity.

- Give an example of a time you transformed a negative thought into a more positive one.

- Share an emotion you are feeling right now.

3. Write a number between 1 and 40 on each of 40 index cards.

4. Hand out copies of the grid to the group participants

B. Directions for group participants

1. Instruct clients to fill each of the circles, in random order, with numbers between 1 and 40 without repeating a number twice.

2. The group leader picks up one index card at a time and reads aloud the number written on it.

3. If the client has the number written in his circle he raises his hand and reads the question in the square. Then he fills in the circle using a colored marker. He must first answer the question in order to fill in the circle, or else he skips his turn.

4. This pattern continues until a participant gets a bingo, i.e., when an individual fills in a row of squares horizontally, vertically, or diagonally.

Discussion: This game has proven very successful in therapy groups. It provides an enjoyable way to review important CBT concepts while encouraging and enhancing socialization, communication, and problem-solving skills. Self-esteem is increased as participants support each other, often helping each other answer questions and positively acknowledging fellow group members who get "Bingo."

Self-worth increases as participants practice concepts that give them strength and greater control in many areas of their life.

NOTES

1. www.beckinstitute.org/cognitive-behavioral-therapy/, accessed on 9 October 2014.

2. www.nami.org/Template.cfm?Section=About_Treatments_and_Supports &template=/ContentManagement/ContentDisplay.cfm&ContentID= 7952, accessed on 9 October 2014.

3. http://psychcentral.com/lib/in-depth-cognitive-behavioral-therapy/ 000907, accessed on 9 October 2014.

4. www.mhcinc.org/poc/view_doc.php?type=doc&id=13024, accessed on 9 October 2014.

5. Dictionary.com – http://dictionary.reference.com/browse/thought?s=ts, accessed on 9 October 2014.

6. Merriam Webster Online Dictionary – www.merriam-webster.com/ dictionary/emotion?show=)&t=1374869362, accessed on 9 October 2014.

7. Merriam Webster Online Dictionary – www.merriam-webster.com/ dictionary/behavior?show=0&t=1396743405, accessed on 9 October 2014.

8. Merriam Webster Online Dictionary – www.merriam-webster.com/ dictionary/emotion?show=0&t=1374869362, accessed on 9 October 2014.

9. www.caleblack.com/psy5493_files/08%20-%20Behavioral%20Activation. pdf, accessed on 9 October 2014.

10. http://ptsd.about.com/od/selfhelp/tp/CommonCBTStrategies.htm, Matthew Tull, PhD, accessed on 9 October 2014.

11. http://ptsd.about.com/od/glossy/g/BAdef.htm, accessed on 9 October 2014.

12. This type of Bingo can be applied to self-esteem: Self-Esteem Bingo, Relationships, Communication and Art Therapy, which is designed in a different manner since drawing in an integral part of it. See Buchalter (2004) in the Bibliography for more details.

CHAPTER 3

Dialectical Behavioral Therapy

Dialectical behavioral therapy (DBT) was created by Marsha Linehan at Washington University in the 1970s.[1] It is an evidenced-based therapy, based on Zen-Buddhist philosophy that has proven highly effective with clients challenged with bipolar disorder. Recently it has come to light that it works well with many clients including individuals suffering from depression, anxiety, eating disorders, and addictions. DBT is beneficial because it validates the client and allows him to play a key role in his therapy. The client works with the therapist to review where he is at the moment and where he wants to be in the future. The client is fully accepted regardless of his past and present issues and experiences. The therapist does not tell the client what to do; instead the therapist and client act as a team. The goal is to work on fulfilling goals and dreams, and finding peace and harmony and a more gratifying and healthy life style.

The therapy is intricate and this introduction will just touch upon some of its main characteristics. Dialectical means that two ideas can both be true at the same time. The client learns that he can like and dislike someone or something simultaneously. For instance, he may like his mother's concern and love, but dislike her authoritarian manner. The individual learns that it is important to think in the abstract and that erroneous thoughts and beliefs, which may include black and white thinking and labeling, are unhealthy and stressful.

In order to think in the abstract and act in a prudent manner the individual would ideally use his wise mind. The wise mind is a combination of reasonable mind and emotional mind. Wise mind is the part of one's thinking where an individual would weigh the outcome of a behavior and decide if it is in his best interest to act upon his impulses. Reasonable mind is the logical side of the mind. It has no emotion and it responds to facts. Emotional mind acts on desires and urges and can easily become out of control. In emotional mind facts maybe be distorted or exaggerated and emotions can become confused and out of control. Yelling, threatening, and punching a hole in the wall would stem from emotional mind.

There are four core functions in DBT. They include mindfulness skills, interpersonal effectiveness skills, emotion regulation skills, and distress tolerance skills. The core mindfulness skills include the wise mind where one learns to observe, describe, participate, be nonjudgmental, and do what works effectively. Interpersonal effectiveness skills are represented by the acronym DEAR MAN. This stands for Describe, Express, Assert, Reinforce, Mindfully (keep your focus), Appear confident, Negotiate.

Included in interpersonal effectiveness is relationship effectiveness and self-respect effectiveness. The acronym here is GIVE, which stands for Gentle, Interested, Validate (the other person), Easy manner. The self-respect effectiveness acronym, FAST, stands for Fair (be fair to yourself and others), Apologies (make no apologies for a request or disagreeing), Stick to values, Truthful.

Emotion regulation skills are symbolized by the acronym PLEASE. This stands for PhysicaL (take care of one's body and health), Eating (balanced diet), Avoiding (non-prescribed mood-altering substances and behaviors), Sleep (balanced), Exercise.

Distress tolerance skills are represented by the acronym Wise Mind ACCEPTS. The word ACCEPTS stands for: Activities, Contributing, Comparisons, Emotions (generating opposite emotion to replace current negative ones), Pushing away (blocking a situation from your mind), Thoughts, Sensations (trying experience intense sensations in order to interfere with the negative emotion being expressed).

Mindfulness is a major focus of DBT. The concept supports individuals to stay in the present moment, not judging their thoughts or actions. Clients are encouraged to be fully aware, tuning into each of their five senses while engaging in one experience/interaction at a time. The individual learns to accept his situation for what it is and not to ruminate or dwell on unpleasant or recurring thoughts.

Self-soothing is an important component of DBT, self-esteem, and stress reduction. It centers on being kind and nurturing to oneself. The acronym is IMPROVE. It stands for Imagery, Meaning (try to find a purpose), Prayer, Relaxation, One thing in the moment, Vacation (giving yourself permission to relax, retreat, accept help) and Encourage (support yourself).

Radical acceptance represents a willingness to accept reality. The client learns that accepting is not the same as approval or giving up. Acceptance helps free individuals from stress and helps them move forward in their life journey. When an individual accepts a situation or illness he can then relinquish himself from the victim role and begin to take control, using his energy to heal and think in a more positive manner.

A behavior chain analysis is a key part of DBT. Marsha Linehan (1993) stated that "the purpose of the behavioral analysis is to figure out what the problem is, what is causing it, what interferes with the resolution of the problem, and what aides are available to help solve the problem."[2] Clients identify a problem or behavior, examine thoughts and feelings associated with it, and look at the costs and benefits of the behavior. On a daily basis they track thoughts, feelings, behaviors, and skills that help them see behavior patterns and identify what works or doesn't work for them.

Art therapy and DBT blend well together. Engaging in art helps individuals focus and become increasingly mindful. Participants are asked not to judge themselves and to allow their artwork to flow from within; it is the creating that is important, not the finished product. Individuals focus on colors, texture, and design while drawing, painting, etc. This helps make the feelings and images become tangible and easier to observe and analyze. As a tool art affords clients the opportunity to understand their patterns of behavior and emotions and to problem solve. For instance, drawing opposite emotions allows clients to view differences in emotions and examine ways to find a balance that is healthy.

DBT teaches skills and increases client motivation for change. Goals are controllable and achievable, measurable and positive, and time focused. Validation greatly helps clients accept themselves so they can engage in constructive transformation. Carl Rogers stated, "The curious paradox is that when I accept myself just as I am, then I can change."

OPPOSITE EMOTION

Materials: Drawing paper, markers, oil pastels, and crayons.

Procedure: Clients fold the paper in half. On one side of the paper they draw an emotion or action and on the other side the opposite emotion or action.

Discussion: Encourage clients to share the two emotions or actions and discuss the behaviors associated with them. Encourage participants to try to focus on the opposite emotion or action when they feel stressed, angry, or depressed. Discuss how "opposite action" can help individuals work through issues, confront situations, deal with distressing emotions, and engage in activities that they might otherwise avoid.

"Opposite Action": according to Dr. Marsha Linehan, "The idea behind this technique is that it can help to deal with distressing emotions by setting into motion an action that is helpful, not harmful. Doing this counteracts the suffering you might otherwise feel because of the distressing emotion. The kinds of situations in which it is appropriate to use this technique are ones in which the emotions might not be realistic to the situation, maybe out of proportion, or escalating, or be emotions that we want to challenge or change."

"Every emotion has an action. If the emotion has an action that means the emotion causes the action. You can actually change the emotion by changing the action. In other words, not only do emotions cause actions, but actions cause emotions. And you can change your emotion by changing your action. So it's kind of a vicious circle—emotions cause actions and then actions cause emotion. And emotions cause actions and actions cause emotions, around and around and around, around, around, around. And the best way to think about it is that emotions love themselves. They just keep themselves going. That's why it's so difficult to change. One of the ways that you can change your emotion is to just reverse the circle. We just start with action that is opposite and that circle starts going in the other way. And the emotion starts going down. Opposite action will work whenever the emotion is not justified by the situation. So that's the basic rule. So the one thing you've always got to figure out is "does the situation actually justify the emotion?"[3]

DISTRESS

Materials: Drawing paper, markers, oil pastels, crayons, pens, pencils, and paint.

Procedure: Clients are asked to represent their stress in the middle of the page, but not taking up the entire page. They may use color, shapes, and figures. Next have them contain it in some way. For example, by drawing a lasso around it or creating another type of barrier. Lastly ask clients to surround their container with a list of ways to better tolerate their stress.

Discussion: Explore emotion regulation strategies. Clients examine their stress and explore characteristics such as the intensity, size, and shape of it. Have them decide if their containment seems sufficient to keep the stress from overwhelming them. Ask questions such as: Has the stress grown over the last few months or years? What do you want to do with the stress and what does the stress do for you? What are its benefits?

EMOTIONS

Materials: Drawing paper, markers, crayons, and oil pastels.

Procedure: Ask participants to do the following: "Close your eyes, take a deep breath and notice your breathing. Let your thoughts come and go and observe how you are feeling: e.g. calm, anxious, angry, frustrated, tense, etc. Don't judge the emotions; let them flow in and out of your awareness. Next draw the emotion that is the strongest. Think about size, movement, shape, color, and perhaps details."

Discussion: Explore the emotion and examine ways to deal with it when it becomes overwhelming. Drawing emotions will enable the artist to gain increased control and power as he becomes creatively in charge of it. The size, shape, placement, and color will create awareness about the power the emotion holds and the work in store for the client in terms of taming it. When the emotion is placed on the paper it becomes easier to identify and the client doesn't "own it" as much. It becomes an entity that is outside of the body instead of inside where it can fester and cause great harm. Encouraging clients to name the emotion, and having them engage in a brief dialogue with it, will help the individual understand more about the emotion, observe it from a variety of perspectives, and begin to gain mastery over it.

DISTRESS TOLERANCE: DREAM VACATION

Materials: Drawing paper, markers, pastels, oil pastels, and crayons.

Procedure: Clients are asked to close their eyes and imagine themselves on a wonderful, relaxing vacation. The place they choose will be well suited to them: a place where they can forget their problems, leave their stress behind, have fun, and focus on their strengths and wishes.

Ask participants to either illustrate the vacation site and/or have them use colors, shapes, and designs to represent the feelings they would experience on this delightful getaway.

Discussion: Vacationing from stress is a coping technique that can be very effective. This practice induces a state of calmness and acceptance, and increases happiness for many individuals. Self-esteem is raised as the client creates and takes control of his vacation. This often generalizes to increased control of emotions, attitudes, and behavior. The individual becomes more optimistic and hopeful.

FIGURE 13

A 77-year-old woman named Francine challenged with a severe depression stemming from the recent death of her husband of 50 years, created her dream vacation. She related the mandala to one she took long ago at a resort in Mexico. She remarked that she used to be young, beautiful, thin, and carefree. "My husband and I traveled all over the world, but Mexico was my favorite place.

I loved to swim and let the sun shine down on me while I napped on a blanket in the sand." Francine shared an incident when her husband poured water on her back while she was napping and shocked her so much she sprinted upright and accidentally knocked him in the nose, which bled for quite some time. She laughed and remarked that her husband didn't think it was funny at the time.

Francine was very focused on the design of the mandala, carefully cutting out the figures and making sure to choose only vibrant-looking men and women. While she was working, Francine spoke about being a model and fashion designer in her youth. She stated she had perfect posture and still took pride in it. She remarked she didn't want to be hunched over like so many older people. Francine shared that she felt relaxed when she imagined the scene she designed. She agreed to visualize it in times of anxiety to reduce stress and remember positive experiences.

ACCEPTANCE ROAD

Materials: Drawing paper, pens, pencils, markers, oil pastels, and crayons.

Procedure: Have clients draw a personalized road and fill it with all the things in their lives that they know they need to accept right now.

Discussion: Acceptance of oneself and one's life situation plays a large part in stress reduction and improved self-esteem. Acceptance does not mean that an individual doesn't work towards self-improvement or special goals; it means acknowledging that certain circumstances, traits, etc. cannot be changed. It means that an individual will probably be healthier and happier if he focuses on what is in his control and not on what is out of his control. People usually become aware that there is a lot more in their control than they thought. For instance, a person may have a disease such as diabetes, which will not go away (out of his control), but that person has control over taking his medication, seeing the doctor regularly, eating nutritiously, and getting enough rest. Acceptance helps individuals tolerate distressing situations and it enables them to "tolerate the moment."

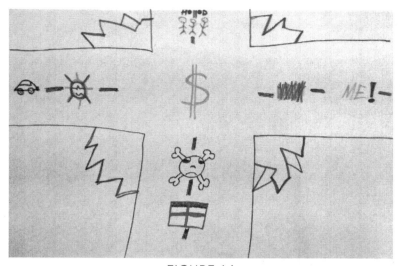

FIGURE 14

Jack, a young man in his 20s challenged with addiction issues and depression, created his own unique acceptance road composed of four intersections. In the middle of the road is a large, gold dollar sign symbolizing his need to accept that money is tight for him right now and he must learn to live within a strict budget. He stated he needs to remember that he shouldn't become depressed (orange scribble on right side of intersection), when he feels financially burdened. The skull and cross bones represent his need to accept his addiction, stop feeling guilty for the trouble he caused his family, and to move on with his life. The car on the left side of the road symbolizes the acceptance that he won't be driving for at least a year because his license was suspended for drink driving. The sun represents hope for a better future and sobriety. Towards the top of the road are three stick figures with the word "Hood" written in letters and symbols. Jack shared that he has to change friends and acquaintances so he is not tempted to take drugs; this is a very difficult task for him.

The corners of the roads have sharp, jagged edges, which represent Jack's need to keep his anger under control. At times he becomes explosive and needs to attend anger management groups to help deal with his aggressive outbursts. Once he accepts his need to attend these groups and works on his sobriety he can begin to form healthier and more productive friendships and relationships. Towards the right of the intersection he writes "ME" with an exclamation point. This represents his need to take control of his life and move on so that he can have a brighter future.

SELF-SOOTHING

Materials: Drawing paper, markers, oil pastels, crayons, pencils, and pens.

Procedure: Begin the session by discussing the value of being independent, treating ourselves in a positive manner, and comforting ourselves. Suggest the clients do not have to wait for others to make them joyful and fulfill their needs; they can do this on their own. For example, they can buy their own cake on their birthday or take themselves out to dinner or to a movie. Next ask clients to draw three hearts. Ask them to fill in each heart with things they do to comfort themselves.

Discussion: Discussion focuses on the size and color of the hearts and the coping skills included. Goals include raising awareness of the importance of self-care and self-nurturance.

OBSERVATION

Materials: Lined writing paper, pens, and pencils.

Procedure: Clients are asked to focus on themselves and everything around them by getting in touch with their immediate environment. Encourage them to list everything they are seeing, hearing, feeling, touching, and perhaps tasting. Ask participants to write down any thoughts that pop into their heads; encourage them to let their thoughts come and go as they please and not to judge them.

Discussion: Clients focus on being mindful and self-aware. They discuss thoughts and feelings, and the benefits of being in the here and now. Discuss how self-esteem is increased when *the mind* has the ability to relax and become calm. Self-awareness assists clients to understand themselves and their reactions to various situations in a clearer, more focused manner. It provides individuals with control, which in turn leads to increased confidence and improved self-esteem.

IDEAL LIFE

Materials: Drawing paper, magazines, glue, scissors, markers, and oil pastels.

Procedure: DBT focuses on living a life that is rewarding, gratifying, and fills our psychological, emotional, and physical needs. Instruct participants to create a collage of their ideal life. They may add words, figures, shapes, places to visit, houses, flowers, lakes, trees, mountains, buildings, etc. They may add their own artwork in addition to the photos.

Discussion: Explore needs and desires and methods of attaining them. Examine differences between how participants are presently living their life and their desired life style. Discuss goals.

BARRIERS

Materials: Drawing paper, markers, and oil pastels.

Procedure: Clients are asked to draw their barrier: meaning what is keeping them from achieving happiness, success, self-fulfillment, good mental health, etc.

Discussion: Participants explore the size and strength of their barrier, when it was first built, how long it has been up, the difficulty or ease of tearing it down, what it looks like, what it's made of, and how it makes them feel, etc.

One client designed a large brick barrier, stating it would never come down. She was afraid that if it did she would lose control and literally fall apart.

WAVES OF EMOTION

Materials: Drawing paper, markers, oil pastels, and crayons.

Procedure: Each individual receives a piece of paper with three pre-drawn waves on it. Ask clients to fill in the waves with colors that represent emotions they are presently experiencing. As an alternative exercise, clients may draw themselves riding an emotional wave, especially if they feel stressed or anxious. They may create the wave themselves.

Discussion: Discussion focuses on the colors used to convey the emotions. Explore the reasons clients feel joyful, sad, angry, etc. Goals include identification and expression of feelings.

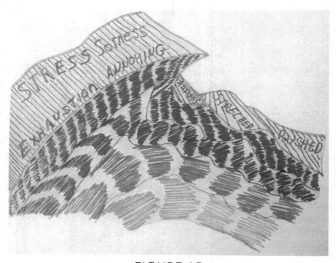

FIGURE 15

Manuel, a young man in his 20s, illustrated various emotional waves. He began at the bottom and worked his way to the crest of the wave. The pink and yellow waves (on the bottom) symbolize the peace he feels when he is home alone or with his long-term girlfriend who is very supportive. The light purple and yellow waves represent his love of art. He remarked that he enjoys drawing and painting, and finds peace when he is experimenting with markers, paint, and pen and ink. He shared that he doesn't consider himself an artist yet but he likes the peace and calm that creativity provides for him. The blue and yellow waves represent his ambivalence about his life. On the one hand he enjoys college and hopes to be a graphic artist, and on the other hand he feels very stressed because he thinks his field will not be lucrative and his parents are pressuring him to get a business degree so he can be financially secure. The purple waves symbolize his increasing anxiety about what to do with his life. The purple waves lead to the top yellow waves, which symbolize, "Stress, sadness, exhaustion, annoying, anxious, pushed, and stretched."

Manuel shared that his goal is to allow the waves to break and to try to become calmer. He stated that money "isn't as important as enjoying life and your job." He is trying to stop his parents from taking control of his life. This is complicated because they are providing all of his financial needs and paying for his schooling and car insurance. While carefully observing his work he decided that the waves are bright and colorful, perhaps representing hope and a light at the end of the tunnel.

FIGURE 16

John, a 30-year-old man challenged with depression and addiction issues, created a man riding the "stress wave." He liked the idea of surfing unpleasant emotions until they subside, and therefore illustrated a man with his arms up, appearing confident and steady. The waves are not too large, appearing relatively smooth, and the sun is out; the birds are flying in the air. A thin red striped border surrounds the surfer to keep him safe but also provides the necessary freedom. Cliff shared he will use this technique when stressed and encouraged his peers to practice it daily.

STRESS RELIEF KIT

Materials: Drawing paper, markers, oil pastels, crayons, and an outline of a large suitcase or old fashioned doctor-type bag (leader can provide the outline by finding an image on Google Images or drawing it herself).

Procedure: Provide an outline to each group member. Suggest they are going to create a stress relief kit. Ask them to draw items needed to fill it (compare it to the medical emergency kits sold that include bandages, antiseptic, etc.). Examples might include:

a relaxation CD, warm milk, a tea bag, photo of grandchildren, mashed potatoes, soft pillow, etc.

Discussion: Discussion focuses on the items included in the kit and the way in which the client will utilize them. Goals include exploration of methods to reduce stress and self-soothe.

THE TURTLE[4]

Materials: Drawing paper, pencils, markers, oil pastels, and colored pencils.

Procedure: Show clients a few photos of turtles and ask them to draw one. Suggest they draw it either inside its shell, or with its head and legs outside of the shell.

Have group members fill in their outline with color and design. Next ask them to write a brief description connecting their illustration to the way they see themselves, "out of their shell?" or "still inside it?"

Discussion: Explore the representations of the turtles and examine the safety aspect of the shell. Ask clients, "How can the shell be a help? How is it a hindrance?" Encourage group members to share their own "shells."

Additional questions may include:

1. How strong is your shell?

2. How large is it?

3. When did it begin growing?

4. How often do you hide in it?

5. What would you like to do with it?

Goals include exploration of fear, inhibitions, and barriers to change.

FIGURE 17

A depressed young woman named Cara designed this despondent turtle she named Tania. Cara shared that the turtle is walking aimlessly in the rain looking for shelter but isn't able to find safety of any sort. She described the turtle as cold, afraid, lonely, and hopeless. The rain (Cara's tears) is falling only on the turtle because "everyone else is happy and the sun shines on all the other turtles, but not on Tania." In the top left of the picture a lightening bolt is lightly drawn. When asked, Cara remarked that the bolt represents anger; "If it strikes Tania she will die." Cara related to the turtle because she feels alone in the world and doesn't believe there is anyone who loves or supports her. She stated her parents and friends are too self focused to care about her.

A group member pointed out that the turtle has a large, strong-looking shell. Cara stated that the shell is protective and she was able to admit that she puts up a barrier very similar to the turtle's shell. It was observed that the turtle appears to be moving forward albeit extremely slowly. Cara commented, "Perhaps Tania will eventually find her way, but I am doubtful." The one time Cara gave a "half smile" was when group members complimented her for her "cute cartoon." Cara did say she loves to draw and that is what helps her survive.

THOUGHTS

Materials: Drawing paper, markers, oil pastel, and crayons.

Procedure: Participants fold their paper in half. They are instructed to spontaneously draw their thoughts on one side of the paper; they are not to censor or judge them. On the other side of the page they draw their thoughts in a controlled manner, placing them in some sort of containment (e.g. circle, square, prison cell, cage, cave, etc.).

Discussion: Explore ways to regulate thoughts and emotions so that the individual learns how to gain better control of his thoughts. The goal is "to not allow your thoughts to control you."

WISE/EMOTIONAL MIND[5]

Materials: Drawing paper, markers, oil pastels, and crayons.

Procedure: Instruct participants to draw their wise mind (balance between reasonable mind and emotional mind) on one half of the page and their emotional mind (thoughts based on feelings, subjective state) on the other half of the page.

Discussion: Examine the similarities and differences between the two drawings. Discuss instances where the emotional mind was dominant and those where the wise mind took charge. Discuss associated emotions and behaviors. Explore ways to create a balance between the *two minds*.

Examine how self-esteem is affected when one side takes charge and how to find a balance.

COLLAGE OF DISTRACTION

Materials: Construction paper, magazine photos, scissors, glue, oil pastels, and markers.

Procedure: Participants are asked to design a collage filled with photos and/or drawings of things they could do to distract themselves when they feel anxious and stressed. Examples include: reading, writing, exercising, listening to music, "creating a collage," etc.

Discussion: Examine methods to divert focus from negative thinking and unproductive behaviors to more positive thinking and behaviors. Explore the benefits of structuring time in a healthy manner and keeping busy.

BALANCE MANDALA

Materials: Drawing paper, paper plates, markers, oil pastels, crayons, paints, brushes, and pencils.

Procedure: Suggest that participants outline a circle from the plate and create *a balance* within the circle. Encourage them to think about ways to represent balance. What would it look like and feel like? What types of colors, designs, figures, and shapes might be utilized?

Discussion: Explore the importance of a balanced life style and how it feels to be in and out of balance. Discuss ways to increase stability and consistency in behavior, attitudes, emotions, relationships, and life style.

SMILING FACES COLLAGE

Materials: Drawing paper, magazine photos, scissors, glue, markers, and pencils.

Procedure: Participants are asked to cut out and glue photos of people smiling. Suggest they choose all types of smiles from full, wide smiles to grins and even "half smiles."[6]

Discussion: Support clients to discuss their reactions to the various facial expressions. Have them examine which photos lift their mood and ask them to share a time when someone's smile changed their attitude or feeling in a positive way. Share research that suggests smiling may change the brain chemistry, stimulating a dopamine response, increasing serotonin and elevating mood. When people smile they are more attractive and usually will receive a better response from others, which in turn raises feelings of self-worth and happiness. Smiling may help improve one's attitude and outlook on life. Examine how facial expressions can play an important role in health and well-being, and in relating to friends and family.

ACCEPTANCE II

Materials: Writing paper, pens, and pencils.

Procedure: Clients create a list of feelings, situations, and emotions they are willing to accept. For instance, their financial situation or a divorce. Next they will be asked to create another list of things they are not ready or willing to accept.

Discussion: Clients explore their attitude, behavior, and reactions towards life events. They are asked to focus on what is in their control instead of dwelling on what is out of their control. In this way they will feel stronger and more successful.

KALEIDOSCOPE

Materials: Drawing paper, markers, crayons, oil pastels, and paints.

Procedure: Explain what a kaleidoscope is and define it.[7] Show group participants pictures of various designs created in the style of a kaleidoscope. (Pictures can be found on Google Images.)

Next suggest that participants create their own kaleidoscope art within the circle.

Discussion: Explore the colors, patterns, and shapes. Examine whether the artist sees anything symbolic in his art such has an image or significant pattern. Discuss the idea of shifting patterns and multiple reflections. Have clients share how these concepts may relate to their life, e.g. change in life style and/or relationships, being able to view situations from many angles and being able to see people and oneself as complex and ever changing.

LIFE BALANCE MANDALA

Materials: Drawing paper, paper plates, markers, crayons, oil pastels, colored pencils, and pens.

Procedure: Suggest that participants outline a circle from the plate and fill in the circle with ways they balance their life style and take care of themselves physically and emotionally. They may refer to the list below for suggestions.

There are many aspects involved in self-care. Some of theses aspects are: physical, spiritual, emotional, intellectual, environmental, leisure, and financial.

Wellness is a balance of the following factors, which contribute to a feeling of well-being:

- **Physical wellness:** getting enough sleep, eating well, exercising, visiting the doctor and getting appropriate tests, not drinking too much alcohol or not at all, not smoking, not drinking too much coffee or soda, being well groomed, exercise reduces stress, helps heart/blood pressure, helps guard against osteoporosis, increases serotonin (feel good chemical in brain), lowers depression, and increases self-esteem, take the stairs instead of the elevator, park far away and walk, make an exercise schedule, dance, stretch, engage in sports, try yoga.

- **Nutrition:** (affects mood, energy level, weight and self-esteem) drink water instead of sugary drinks, eat small meals throughout the day so you don't get too hungry, eat breakfast, limit processed carbohydrates (e.g. eat wheat instead of white bread), eat more vegetables, fruit, chicken and fish, don't eat two to three hours before bed, eat at least five to seven servings of fruit and vegetables each day, try small energy boosters such as peanut butter on crackers or celery, other healthy snacks include: hummus and rice cakes or pitta chips, or egg whites on wheat toast.

- **Spiritual wellness:** searching for meaning in our life, spirituality doesn't have to focus on religion, it can be the belief in a higher power or nature, family, music, art—you decide, it is something to believe in that gives you a purpose, hope and/or inspiration.

- **Stress reduction:** meditation, mindfulness—being in the moment, deep breathing, prayer, positive self-talk, exercise, yoga, creativity/art, dance/movement, creative writing.

Discussion: Focus on the importance of understanding one's needs and necessities and finding healthy ways to achieve them. When one's world is in harmony he is usually brighter, more motivated and his self-esteem is raised. Relationships in all areas improve and energy is increased.

THOUGHT PATTERNS

Thought patterns: Habit of thinking in a particular way or making certain assumptions, usually positive or negative.[8]

Materials: Drawing paper, markers, oil pastels, and crayons.

Procedure: Have the participants draw distorted thought patterns on one side of the paper and organized thought patterns on the other.

Discussion: Observe the intensity, severity and repeat of patterns as well as the organization or disorganization of patterns. Explore the artwork to help identify the impact that thought patterns have on self-esteem, self-awareness, attitude, and overall functioning.

THE LIFE JACKET

Materials: Drawing paper, scissors, glue, marker, oil pastels, and crayons.

Procedure: Each group member receives a photo of a life jacket or they may draw their own life jacket. Participants are asked to glue the photo somewhere on the page. Next they are asked to draw, write and/or find pictures from magazines to represent ways in which their life jacket may protect them and keep them "afloat." Suggest that the life jacket may include people, items, thoughts, the environment, and behaviors. Examples may include: family, friends, coping skills such as deep breathing, and attitudes such as optimism.

Discussion: Explore distraction techniques, various methods to avail oneself of help, how to nurture a support system, and how to become self reliant. Examine techniques to self-soothe.

"The Life Jacket Metaphor" is central to "The Decider." The concept: that each skill helps to inflate the life jacket. The client recognizes when they are in a situation for which the use of skills could prove useful. They are able to use the skills if an 'emotional emergency' occurs. This enables the client to float rather than sink when it seems they are drowning in a sea of distressing emotion."[9]

THE WALL

Materials: Drawing paper, markers, oil pastels, and crayons.

Procedure: Participants are asked to draw a wall or barrier separating them from their problem, feeling, anxiety, or negative thoughts.

They will draw a symbol or image representing themselves, a wall, and their problem or feeling.

Discussion: The wall may be used as a distraction when problems and fears become overwhelming and when individuals begin obsessing about worries and fears. Sometimes individuals need a vacation from their problems and creating a wall has its benefits when it is used for protection from stress and anxiety. The more control individuals have over their wall the stronger they will be and the better they will feel about their self-worth. The goal is to be able to put the wall up when needed and to have the strength to tear it down when the time is appropriate. The wall becomes negative only when it blocks us from our feelings and emotions all the time. Self-awareness regarding one's wall is crucial.

When the wall is completed, encourage individuals to describe feelings associated with it. Have them think about its size, color, shape, and strength. Questions asked may include:

1. How can you use the wall to distract yourself when stressed?

2. What are its benefits?

3. When would it be particularly helpful to use it?

4. How long has it been up?

5. How long do you think it will stay up?

6. Do you wish it would change in any way in future weeks, months, years, etc.?

FIGURE 18

Christopher, a young man in his 20s, created a tall brick wall leaning slightly to the left. Christopher stated his wall helped him lessen feelings of guilt associated with his heroin addiction and his history of telling lies and stealing from his family in order to purchase drugs. He stated his guilt can be overwhelming and the shame he feels may provide him with an excuse to keep using; therefore, he has to continue working on leaving the past behind and working towards a clean and healthier future. On the left side of the wall, Christopher portrays himself feeling well and trying to move on with his life. He is also placed on top of the wall aiming a bow and arrow, ready to shoot at all of the concerns that might harm him. He places the negatives in his life in bubbles to contain them. They include: fear, regret, hopelessness, self-hatred, lack of motivation and more fear. He includes fear four times. Christopher stated he thinks he can overcome the obstacles but needs the wall for protection. He shared that he hopes the wall stays sturdy and he doesn't fall off of it. When asked how long the wall had been up, Christopher remarked that although it is strong and tall, it was recently built and still vulnerable to outside forces. He did say he thinks it will remain standing for a long time, "As long as I need it."

RADICAL ACCEPTANCE

Materials: Drawing paper, markers, oil pastels, and crayons.

Procedure: Share the following description with group members:
"You are at the edge of a steep cliff. Down below is a deep blue river surrounded by mountains that tower over it. Thick clumps of leaves protruding from tree branches grow off the cliff. The sun is high in the sky and you smell the fragrance of wild flowers overgrown and roaming endlessly near the mountain. You know it is time to take the plunge. Draw what happens next."

Discussion: Marsha Linehan provides this metaphor for radical acceptance: "Radical acceptance is not simply a cognitive stance or cognitive activity; it is a total act. It is jumping off a cliff. You must keep jumping over and over because you can only accept in this one moment. Therefore, you have to keep actively accepting, over and over again in every moment.

If radical acceptance is jumping off a cliff into the deep abyss, then there is always a tree stump coming out of the cliff just below the top and the minute you fall past you reach out and cling onto that stump. And then you're on another cliff's edge, asking perhaps, "How did this happen?" Then, you jump off the cliff again.

Radical acceptance is the constant jumping off, jumping off, jumping off and jumping off, yet again. Radical acceptance is also the nonjudgmental acceptance of the repeated grabbing onto the tree stump."[10]

Analyze the presentation of the picture. Explore how it felt to jump over the cliff. Did the figure plunge into the water; did he hang onto a branch? Was he hesitant about jumping or did he jump without thinking about it? What happened if he fell into the water? Did he swim? Did he drown, etc.? Discuss the effect radical acceptance has on our feelings, attitudes, and behavior. Share how accepting the inevitable and going with Marsha Linehan's flow increases happiness and lessens stress. Discuss the definition of radical acceptance: "letting go of fighting reality. Accepting your situation for what it is."

STONES

Materials: A variety of stones with interesting textures; pens, markers, pastels, crayons, and drawing/writing paper are optional.

Procedure: The group leader presents a box or basket of stones to group members and asks everyone to choose one stone. Participants are asked to examine their stone and describe it in detail focusing on color, size, shape, texture, feel, etc.

Another option is to have participants sketch their stone and describe both their sketch and the actual stone. In this way they analyze the stone even more carefully. They may also write about the stone in detail.

Discussion: Group members describe their experience and the intricacies of the stone. The importance of being mindful and observant in order to feel peaceful and focused is explored.

HALF SMILE[10]

Materials: Drawing paper, markers, oil pastels, crayons, and template of a head and neck if desired.

Procedure: Suggest that participants draw a face with a half smile, which is a mouth turned up just slightly. Next ask group members to write a sentence or two about the reason for the half smile.

Discussion:

Even the simulation of an emotion tends to arouse it in our minds.

—*Charles Darwin*

According to Marsha Linehan, the pioneer of DBT, "this act alone, this change in body language, has proven to have a positive effect on your body's chemicals and neurotransmitters." Encourage clients to try the half smile and practice doing this a few times a day. Discuss how our attitude and body language can play a positive role in recovery from depression and other illnesses. "A half smile is slightly upturned lips with a relaxed face. Try to adopt a serene facial expression. Remember, your body communicates to your mind."

LOVE DANDELIONS

Materials: Drawing paper, markers, pens, pencils, outlines of dandelions to fill in, scissors, and glue.

Procedure: Read the following description of a dandelion, written by Cathy Moonshine. Next have clients draw at least three dandelions or fill in the outlines of three dandelions, which the group leader will provide. Have participants cut out their dandelions and paste them onto another sheet of paper to create a pleasing arrangement. Next to each dandelion ask participants to list habits or behaviors that are problematic, and are difficult or impossible to be eliminated.

"This is a metaphor about how the more you try to control something the more it may control you. In gardening the plants that are the most resilient are the weeds; in the lawn it's the dandelions that are the most resilient. You could spend a lot of time and energy trying to rid the lawn of the dandelions, but you will probably still have dandelions. Obsessing about getting rid of all dandelions can significantly lower your quality of life.

Individuals have dandelions in their lives. Dandelions are traits, habits, or behaviors that are problematic, but can't be completely eliminated. An example of a personal dandelion is addiction. Someone with an addiction can get into recovery; however, they have to work on a daily basis to not return to their addictive life style. Other dandelions could be self-harm behavior, difficulties with food, being reactive, wanting to win, and perfectionism, among others. It is essential to identify your dandelions to develop effective strategies to manage them."[11]

Discussion: Explore the issues and encourage clients to discuss ways to cope with their dandelions. Questions such as: 'How many dandelions do you have?' or 'How resilient are your dandelions?' may be explored.

TURNING THE MIND I

Materials: Drawing paper, markers, oil pastels, crayons, magazine photos, scissors, and glue.

Procedure: Ask participants to draw and/or use magazine photos to represent something they need to accept. Represent it, whether through drawing, collage or specific images over and over again as reinforcement. They should think of Andy Warhol's pattern art as an example (e.g. the Campbell's Soup cans on canvas in particular) when repeating the image.

Discussion: The following material was taken from the work of Dr. Marsha Linehan.

"Acceptance of reality as it is requires an act of CHOICE.[12]

It is like coming to a fork in the road. You have to turn your mind towards the acceptance road and away from the rejecting reality road.

You have to make an inner COMMITTMENT to accept."

Driving analogy: "you are in the driver's seat with how to respond to your thoughts, feelings, and behaviors. You can decide which road you are driving on. If the current road is not effective, you may turn right, left, make a U-turn, or pull over."[13]

"Focus on understanding when you are emotionally activated, take a moment to pause, and consider all your options. After consideration, you may want to act upon the one that is most effective."

"Turning the mind is that interior turn where you simply say, 'Yes. I will. OK.' It means you find within yourself the ability to say 'Every moment is perfect. Every day is a good day. Everything is as it should be.' It may not be what you want, but it's what it should be. It's just that turning of the mind."[14]

Trying to control things to be the way *we* want them doesn't work.

"When we realize that we are not, as I like to call it, 'Directors of the Universe,' we can begin to see all of the wasted energy we put into trying to orchestrate and control everything happening around us. While we do have control over which decisions *we* make, as we know, there are many other variables that we cannot, including the past, and to a large extent, other people's actions. The sooner we learn and accept this and live accordingly, the sooner we can reduce unnecessary suffering in our lives."

"The Universe is much larger than any catastrophe [in our lives]."

"When it comes to being willing and radically accepting the moment, we must turn the mind again and again, because it will naturally resist and doubt. It's a natural process for the mind, and in turning the mind, we retrain our way of thinking toward acceptance and peace."[15]

BOAT/ANCHOR

Materials: Drawing paper, glue, scissors, construction paper, magazine photos, markers, oil pastels, and crayons.

Procedure: Read Dr. Marsha Linehan's metaphor to group members:

"Your mind is like a boat that is tied to a chain with an anchor. Mindfulness is the anchor and chain that gently pull the boat (your attention) back each time the waves start to carry it away. Even if your mind wanders off 1,000 times, you've done the exercise if you gently pull your attention back to your point of focus. There's no right or wrong to it. All that matters is paying attention to your experience while you do the exercise as well as you can. You can do this type of practice with anything you care to bring your full and undivided attention to. In doing so, you'll learn a lot about yourself, about other people, and about any situation in which you find yourself. And, just like a muscle that gets stronger and stronger with exercise, your capacity to move your attention to what you want it to focus on will grow strong."

Ask participants to draw a boat connected to an anchor and chain in any way they desire. The images may be realistic or abstract. Cut paper may be used as well as magazine photos.

Discussion: Examine the benefits of "not judging" attitudes, thoughts, or abilities. Discuss how mindfulness allows individuals the freedom to "be themselves." Explore the connection between the mind, boat, and anchor. Explore the size of the boat and anchor and the ease or difficulty of keeping the boat (mind) in tow.

QUIETING THE MIND

Materials: Drawing paper, markers, oil pastels, and crayons.

Procedure: Ask participants to write the word "peace" in a way that symbolizes tranquility and serenity, thinking of serene colors and shapes. They can then design a background around the word.

Next do a brief meditation, by reading the following to the group:

> Sit in a comfortable position. Close eyes and breathe deeply in a slow and relaxed manner. Pay attention to your breathing. Block out all other thoughts and sensations. Keep your attention on your breathing. As you inhale say the word "peace" to yourself and as you exhale say the word "calm." Continue this exercise for a few minutes.

Discussion: Encourage clients to describe their artwork and the peace derived from the relaxation exercise. Ask them to work together to create a list of stress-reducing activities.

BUILDING A LIFE WORTH LIVING

Materials: Pens, pencils, drawing paper, markers, colored pencils, oil pastels, magazine photos, glue, and scissors.

Procedure: Group members are asked to draw and/or create a collage of what "Your life worth living" would look like. Examples to use may include: food, love, a house, family, health symbols, electronics, friends, and nature, etc. Participants may add as many images as they please. When they have completed the artwork they may write their answers to the questions below or the questions may just be discussed verbally.

Discussion:

1. Describe what is included in your "life worth living."

2. How can you fill your life with these items, people, feelings, things, etc.?

3. What gets in the way of your "life worth living?" (Specify barriers.)

4. How can you minimize or eliminate your barriers?

5. What else can you do to continue to develop a life worth living? (E.g. develop new hobbies, new goals, etc.)

6. Have you ever lived your ideal life? What was it like?

7. If you have never lived your ideal life, describe what it would be like.

THIS MOMENT

Materials: Magazine photos, drawing paper, markers, oil pastels, and crayons.

Procedure: Ask participants to close their eyes for a few moments and imagine themselves somewhere they feel comfortable, safe, and content. Next have them represent this special place on paper in any way they please.

Discussion: Explore this unique place and the feelings it elicits. Discuss ways to duplicate the serenity experienced while drawing. Share the importance of taking a mental vacation periodically throughout the day.

TURNING THE MIND II[16]

Materials: Drawing paper, markers, pens and pencils, markers, magazines, scissors, and glue.

Procedure: Give participants the following instructions: "Draw two roads. On the first road draw the road you take when you are being ineffective, having problems, or damaging relationships. Label what thoughts, feelings, and behaviors you are engaging in along this road. Now draw the road that you can take to be more effective. Label what thoughts, feelings, and behaviors you are engaging in along this road."

Discussion: Explore coping techniques and patterns of thinking and behavior. Focus upon self-awareness.

NOTES

1. www.dbtselfhelp.com/html/what_is_dbt_.html, accessed on 9 October 2014.

2. http://blogs.uw.edu/brtc/files/2013/03/Behavioral-Analysis.pdf, accessed on 9 October 2014.

3. www.dbtselfhelp.com/html/opposite_action_part_1.html, accessed on 9 October 2014.

4. Project taken from an idea by Cathy Moonshine, PhD, MAC, CADC lll, Dialectical Behavior, PESI, LLC, Eau Claire, Wisconsin 2008. If it appears too difficult for clients to draw the turtle, two outlines might be distributed, one with the turtle inside its shell and the other with it displaying its head and legs. The clients may then choose one of the outlines and fill it in.

5. "Wise, reasonable and emotional mind" coined by Marsha Linehan.

6. Dr Marsha Linehan coined the term "half smile."

7. Wikipedia: A **kaleidoscope** is a circle of mirrors containing loose, colored objects such as beads or pebbles and bits of glass. As the viewer looks into one end, light entering the other end creates a colorful pattern, due to the reflection off the mirrors. (http://en.wikipedia.org/wiki/Kaleidoscope, accessed on 9 October 2014.)

8. www.oxforddictionaries.com/us/definition/american_english/thought-pattern?q=thought-pattern

9. Life jacket concept taken from www.thedecider.org.uk/about.html, accessed on 9 October 2014.

10. Radical acceptance metaphor written by Marsha Linehan. http://storyandantistory.org/2007/06/marsha-linehans-wonderful-metaphor-for-radical-acceptance/, accessed on 9 October 2014. Hayes, S.C., Jacobsen, N.S., Follette, V.M. and Dougher, M.J. (1994) *Acceptance and Change: The Central Dialectic in Psychotherapy*. Reno, NV: Contect Press.

11. Cathy Moonshine, PhD, MAC, CADC lll (2008) *Acquiring Competency and Achieving Proficiency with Dialectical Behavior Therapy, Volume ll The Worksheets*. Eau Claire WI: Pesi.

12. www.borderlinepersonality.ca/dbtdistress4.htm, accessed on 9 October 2014.

13. http://byronclinic.com.au/Accepting%20Reality%20-%20From%20DBT%20workshop.pdf, accessed on 9 October 2014.

14. www.dhs.wisconsin.gov/mh_bcmh/confandtraining/SixSlidesPerPage DBTPart%20II.pdf (page 3), accessed on 9 October 2014.

15. http://askdrcliff.com/archives/1245, accessed on 9 October 2014.

16. www.my-borderline-personality-disorder.com/2012/09/turning-the-mind-mindfulness-dbt-accepting-past.html

CHAPTER 4

Mindfulness

Mindfulness is an integral part of therapy because it helps the client to experience peace and serenity. Mindfulness has origins in Eastern philosophy and Buddhism, but individuals do not need to be religious or even spiritual to practice it. According to Jon Kabat-Zinn, "Mindfulness means paying attention in a particular way; on purpose, in the present moment, and non judgmentally."[1] "Mindfulness is about observation without criticism; being compassionate with yourself. In essence, mindfulness allows you to catch negative thought patterns before they tip you into a downward spiral. It begins the process of putting you back in control of your life."[2] Mindfulness is a way of observing our experience, in the present moment, without judgment. Mindfulness helps us "defuse"—to distance ourselves from unhelpful thoughts, reactions, and sensations.[3]

When an individual is mindful he is in the moment and fully aware of his senses and experiences. The client is encouraged not to judge his thoughts, feelings, and behaviors. He doesn't dwell on the past or on feelings of guilt. Individuals are encouraged to focus their full attention on what they are experiencing in the moment and to let their incoming thoughts gently flow away. Attention, or awareness, is the central ingredient feature of mindfulness. "Mindfulness is a skill that allows us to be less reactive to what is happening in the moment. It is a way of relating to all experience—positive, negative, and neutral—such that our overall suffering is reduced and our sense of well-being increases."[4]

Core features of mindfulness include observing, describing, participating fully, being non-judgmental, and focusing on one thing at a time.

Mindfulness can include techniques such as deep breathing, focusing on your breath, observing your thoughts, and creative techniques such as drawing a flower in detail or listening to music. It might incorporate methods such as staring at an object to view it fully. It might comprise being aware of all your senses at one time. Mindfulness practice is about learning to control your own mind, rather than your mind controlling you.

Mindfulness improves both mental and physical health. It reduces anxiety and helps individuals find pleasure in life. It lessens worries and regrets, and helps people enjoy relationships and activities. Self-esteem increases as worry about what others think diminishes and control over one's life increases. Pain and obsessive thoughts often seem to decrease.

Focusing on the moment generates energy and clear-headedness and might help individuals develop new habits that help to weaken negative patterns of thinking and behavior. Over time, mindfulness brings about long-term changes in mood and levels of happiness and well-being.

Art therapy works well as a mindfulness technique because being engaged in creative endeavors helps the individual focus on the artwork, which becomes his center of consciousness. He is in the moment, aware only of color, line, image, and design. He is not judging his work, but allowing his art to flow from within.

THE SUN

Materials: Drawing paper, markers, pastels, oil pastels, and crayons.

Procedure: Ask clients to close their eyes and imagine that a large bright sun is shining its rays down on them. Ask them to think about the warmth and feel of the rays. Suggest that the rays are penetrating all body parts: their head, face, neck, shoulders, back, arms, stomach, legs, feet, and toes. Ask group members to feel the healing warmth and soothing comfort the sun provides. Next suggest clients draw either the sensation of healing, their body as it becomes healthier, and/or the sun emitting its rays.

Discussion: Examine the verbal and creative responses to the imagery. Discuss how positive thinking and "warm" feelings affect the body and mind. Explore ways clients can nurture themselves. Goals include increased involvement of the client with regards to self-soothing, stress reduction, and recovery.

MINDFULNESS

Materials: Drawing paper, markers, and colored pencils.

Procedure: Ask clients to divide their paper into six boxes or provide a sheet already divided. At the top of each box they write one of the following statements:

> Box 1: Focus on your breathing

> Box 2: Focus on nature (beauty, fragrance)

> Box 3: Listen carefully to others

> Box 4: Enjoy a warm shower or bath (become aware of sensations)

> Box 5: Focus on your food (texture, smell, taste)

> Box 6: Love yourself unconditionally (accept yourself for who you are)

Next suggest individuals illustrate each statement using colors, shapes, and/or figures.

Discussion: Discussion focuses on the mindfulness suggestions and the associated images. Suggest clients share other ideas and techniques that allow them to focus and be present. Share the importance of mindfulness as a way to decrease stress, lower blood pressure, "be in the moment," maintain a more positive attitude, and enjoy life.

In one session using this activity clients were able to fully engage in this creative experience although they needed a few minutes to fully understand the concept. Examples of illustrations included a drawing of a pizza pie to represent "focus on food." The client remarked that if she focused hard enough she could actually smell the aroma of the pizza fresh out of the oven. Many clients drew their home shower to represent "enjoy a warm bath or shower," and mentioned how lovely and soothing the warm water feels on their backs. Flowers and trees were often drawn to represent nature. Clients were able to share thoughts about the fresh smell of newly cut grass and the beautiful fragrances of various flowers. Most individuals drew themselves to represent "love yourself unconditionally." They shared the importance of self-acceptance and the difficulty they have with it. Group members appeared to enjoy illustrating their breathing by using wavy lines and simple shapes. One woman drew a mouth with air blowing out of it. A brief breathing exercise that related to the drawings proved beneficial to clients and ended the session in a positive manner.

MINDFULNESS EXERCISE

Materials: Paper, pastels, crayons, and markers.

Method: Ask patients to close their eyes and relax, and listen to the sounds around them (birds chirping, sounds from the heater or air conditioner, wind blowing, etc.). Ask them to focus on the sounds and let all other thoughts float away. After a few minutes suggest that they draw what they experienced. They may use color and shape, or objects and figures to represent their thoughts and feelings.

Discussion: Discussion focuses on the importance of becoming mindful in one's life. The importance of taking time to stop *and smell the roses*, not dwelling on the past or worrying about the future, may be explored.

Goals include stress reduction and relaxation.

INNER PEACE COLLAGE

Materials: Construction paper, scissors, glue, collage materials such as magazines, pom-poms, feathers, sequins, a variety of textiles, and glitter.

Procedure: Ask clients to take a few deep breaths and then close their eyes and listen to tranquil music for a few minutes. Suggest they relax their bodies and try to free their minds from all other thoughts. Next have them create a collage representative of the peace they felt while they were listening to the music.

Discussion: Discussion focuses on the peaceful thoughts and feelings and the symbolism represented in the collage. Goals include self-awareness, mindfulness, relaxation, self-soothing and stress reduction.

MINDFUL DRAWING

Materials: Drawing paper, markers, oil pastels, watercolors, crayons, watercolor crayons, and soothing music.

Procedure: Encourage group members to listen to the music and relax. Ask them to take a few deep, cleansing breaths. Direct them to use markers, pastels, crayons, and/or watercolors to create illustrations that relate to one or more of the themes listed below. Suggest they feel free to experiment with shape, line, and color. Have them "think about the flow of the lines and the feelings elicited by the calming scenes."

- a day at the beach

- floating on a cloud

- a walk in the park

- relaxing at home

- swimming in a lake or pool

- walking in moist, cool sand

- sitting in the grass, feeling the warm sun shine on you

- watching snowflakes gently fall to the earth

- watching a baby sleep peacefully

- flowers swaying in the breeze

- a waterfall in the rainforest

- a sunset or sunrise

- tropical island

- relaxing on a sailboat

- sitting in a comfortable chair by a fireplace

- reclining in a float or in a pool

- a rainbow after a summer shower.

Discussion: Encourage group members to share their associations to the illustrations and explore peaceful sensations. Emphasize the importance of having a variety of relaxing imagery to utilize when anxiety becomes problematic. Goals include relaxation, focusing, and being mindful.

PEACEFUL MIND

Materials: Drawing paper, markers, oil pastels, crayons, and pastels.

Procedure: Instruct clients to write the word "peace" in a way that symbolizes its meaning: tranquility and serenity. Suggest they think of serene colors and shapes to add to the word design. When the exercise is completed ask them to try to find their "peace" by listening to the following brief meditation:

"Sit in a comfortable position. Close your eyes and breathe deeply in a slow and relaxed manner. Pay attention to your breathing. Block out all other thoughts and sensations. Keep your attention on your breathing. As you inhale say the word 'peace' to yourself and as you exhale say the word 'calm.' Continue this exercise for a few minutes."

Have clients describe their artwork and the peaceful feelings derived from the relaxation exercise. Lastly, ask them to work together to create a list of stress-reducing activities. This directive might take up to two sessions depending on the length of the sessions and the abilities of group members.

Discussion: Goals include the exploration of relaxing activities and an introduction to mindfulness and other methods to reduce stress.

THE SENSES

Materials: Drawing paper, markers, oil pastels, and crayons.

Procedure: Suggest that group members would benefit from becoming more cognizant of their surroundings. Ask them to take two deep cleansing breaths and then have them close their eyes for a minute or two. Direct clients to focus on any sounds they may hear. Next ask them to open their eyes and look carefully around the room. Instruct them to observe texture, shape, design, and color. Next instruct clients to draw or write their answers to the following:

- List the colors you see.

- List the sounds you hear.

- List any scents you smell.

- What is the temperature like in the room?
- List at least three items you see.
- Describe how your clothes feel against your skin.
- How is your body feeling? (e.g. headache, arthritis, stomach rumblings, etc.).

Discussion: Clients explore their surroundings in order to become mindful, decrease anxiety, clear their mind, and learn to focus. Goals include stress reduction and self-awareness.

COMFORT COLLAGE

Materials: Drawing paper, magazines, markers, scissors, and glue.

Procedure: Provide group members with a sheet of drawing paper that has a picture of a rocking chair in the middle. Briefly discuss the comforting feeling one may experience by rocking gently. Next ask clients to select additional photos of people, places, and things that are conducive to feeling comfortable and relaxed. Examples include someone napping, relaxing in an easy chair, floating in pool, petting a dog, etc.

Discussion: Explore methods to relieve stress and feel physically soothed. Goals include self-care and focusing on mindfulness.

THE OCEAN: A RELAXATION EXERCISE

Materials: Drawing paper, markers, oil pastels, pastels, and crayons.

Procedure: Have clients share reasons they like to go to the seashore. Then ask them to draw their interpretation of the seashore including items or things that make them feel relaxed. Suggest to clients this is a stress-reducing exercise; they may want to visualize themselves relaxing on the sand, on the boardwalk or in the water while they draw. They may use pastels to gently spread the color and represent the feeling of the seashore. Soothing background music may be played as an additional stress reducer.

Discussion: Discussion focuses on the feelings elicited while drawing and the symbolism portrayed. Goals include stress reduction, focusing on positive imagery and self-soothing.

Clients usually create a list of reasons they like to visit the ocean. In recent groups clients created the following list: "Tranquil, waves, freedom, cool water, sand, birds, the sound of the sea, seagulls, watching dolphins in Cape May, watching boats go by, salty fresh air, hypnotizing waves, especially at night, soft sand, 'reminds me of childhood,' warm, squishy mud, people smiling, watching children playing in the sand."

MIND JAR[5]

Materials: Glitter glue, hot water, Mason jar or bottle, food coloring if desired, one cup hot water, and a stick to swirl liquid.

Procedure: Give the group members the following instructions: "Put one cup of hot water into the jar, then put about two tablespoons of glitter glue and a few drops of food coloring into the jar. Whisk the concoction to break up the glitter glue. Add fine glitter until there is about a ½ to ¾ inch (2.5 × 8 cm) layer on the bottom. Fill the jar with water, leave about 1 inch at the top for shaking room. Place the lid on tight and shake it. The mixture settles after approximately two or three minutes."

Discussion: A mind jar is a jar full of glitter glue, glitter, and water. The idea is to swirl it around and relax as you watch the glitter fall to the bottom of the jar. Sometimes even a few moments of relaxation and focusing can increase energy and quiet the mind.

ONE MINUTE BREATHING/ONE MINUTE PAINTING

Materials: Watercolor paper, watercolor paints, brushes, and water.

Procedure: Group members are asked to:

1. inhale for 20 seconds

2. hold the breath for 20 seconds

3. exhale for 20 seconds.

They do this exercise three times and then paint how it feels to hold in their breath on one side of the page and to breathe out on the other side.

Discussion: Explore feelings associated with holding in one's breath and then releasing the breath slowly. Relate the breathing exercise to the benefits of allowing feelings to emerge and not bottling them up.

MINDFUL LISTENING I

Materials: A variety of music and songs.

Procedure: Have an array of music to play for clients. Ask them to listen without judgment and to allow their thoughts to wander along with the music. They may close their eyes if desired.

Discussion: Participants explore feelings and associations elicited by the music. The impact music has on one's mood and emotional state is explored.

MINDFUL LISTENING II

Materials: Watercolor paper, watercolors, brushes, and an array of relaxing music.

Procedure: Explain to participants: "Listen to the music and relax. Take a few deep, cleansing breaths. Use markers, pastels, crayons, and/or watercolors to create illustrations that relate to one or more of the themes listed below. Feel free to experiment with shape, line, and color. Think about the flow of the lines and the feelings elicited by the calming scenes."

- a day at the beach
- floating on a cloud
- a walk in the park
- relaxing at home
- swimming in a lake or pool
- walking in wet, cool sand
- sitting in the grass, feeling the warm sun shine on you
- watching snowflakes gently fall to the earth
- watching a baby sleep
- flowers swaying in the breeze
- a waterfall
- a sunset or sunrise
- tropical island
- relaxing on a sailboat
- sitting in a comfortable chair by a fireplace
- reclining in a float in a pool.

Discussion: Explore the music, themes, and images elicited by the music. Discuss the impact that creative expression through art and music has on calming the mind and stress reduction.

WIND, TREE, SKY

Materials: Drawing paper, markers, oil pastels, crayons, and paper plates.

Procedure: Play soft, soothing music and take participants through a brief guided imagery. Encourage group members to close their eyes and sit in a relaxed position, and to imagine they are sitting in a comfortable chair, enjoying a warm, beautiful summer day: "The birds are singing and there is calming stillness. The comforting sound of flowing water is heard from a nearby stream and the sound of leaves rustling in the wind is like music to the ears. The air smells fresh and sweet. Breathing it in cleanses your soul. The branches and leaves on the trees are gently swaying in the breeze. A small brown squirrel is scurrying up one of the branches. A cardinal with a bright red breast is perched high on an evergreen. All is well in the world. The sun is warm, but not too hot. It is sending healing rays that penetrate your body. You can feel the warmth in your face, chest, arms, and legs. The healing warmth is flowing through your veins and into your blood stream. It is making you healthy, vital and strong. You feel at one with nature and you are at peace."

Keep the music playing and allow clients to contemplate the imagery for a few minutes. Then ask them to create a mandala that represents the feelings they experienced. Have them include at least one tree and a representation of the wind and sky in the mandala.

Discussion: Explore the peacefulness attained during the guided imagery and while designing the mandala. Examine ways to experience serenity at home. Discuss how participants relate to the key symbols (tree, sky, and wind) and to the power and beauty of nature.

LOVING BREATH

Materials: Drawing paper, pastels, crayons, and markers.

Procedure: Suggest that clients slowly breathe in and out and imagine their breath is embracing them. Explain that they are being "bathed in peace, love, and warmth." Suggest they breathe in beauty and calmness, and breathe out comfort and solace. After this exercise ask clients to draw themselves being embraced by something or someone they love.

Discussion: Discussion focuses on how clients felt during the exercise, and the way they designed their drawing. Encourage them to share how it feels to be embraced, and explore whom or what embraced them in their mandala. Goals include exploration of ways to achieve inner peace and feelings of comfort.

BODY SCAN

Materials: Drawing paper, pastels, crayons, and markers.

Procedure: Lead group members in a full body scan. Have them close their eyes (if they are comfortable doing so) and suggest they relax their eyebrows, eyes, nose, mouth, jaw, neck, shoulders, arms, hands, chest, stomach, thighs, legs, feet, and toes. Go through each body part slowly and in a soft, low voice. Soothing music may be playing as you do this. After the exercise ask group members to draw a line through the mandala separating it in half. Suggest they draw how their body felt before the exercise on one side of the mandala, and how their body felt after the exercise on the other side of it.

Discussion: Discussion may focus on how the artwork reflects the relaxation experience and the changes that occurred during the exercise. Goals include learning how to self-soothe and de-stress in order to attain a peaceful state of being and to help ward off anxiety and panic attack

MINDFULNESS FLOWER

Materials: Drawing paper, markers, oil pastels, and crayons.

Procedure: Group members are asked to draw a flower composed of a small circle in the center and at least six outer petals filling the page of a 9 × 12 inches (22 × 30 cm) or larger sheet of paper. They are instructed to write their name in the center circle and the names of people who are supportive and who they admire, love, or like on the petals. Next participants have the option of further decorating the flower to add color and life to it. Group members share the significance and outstanding traits of the people they included on the petals. Lastly clients participate in a brief guided imagery. This meditation can be led by a group leader or on one's own to enhance a feeling of peace and love:

"Close your eyes and take a deep cleansing breath (in through your nose and out through your mouth). Focus on your breathing for a few seconds, letting your thoughts float through your mind as they come and go. Concentrate on the center of the flower (you). Visualize the circular shape, colors, and fragrance. Notice the texture and beauty of the center, how it is distinctive, an amazing gift of nature. Now focus on the first petal (remember the petals are composed of people who provide support and warmth). Imagine a soft, silky, hair thin petal gently folding towards you, covering you with beauty, peace, and harmony. Feel how it lightly brushes against your skin, creating an immediate feeling of well-being and tenderness. Next visualize the second petal, equally magnificent, covering you gently with its lovely embrace. The third petal begins its descent, slowly finding its way towards the center as if engaging in a fine choreographed ballet, then the fourth petal gingerly joins in, then the fifth petal begins its descent, and the last petal, the sixth petal, elegantly completes the circle. Now you are lightly covered, safe and warm, swaddled like an infant in a secure, tender nest, surrounded by those who only want the best for you: people who are there for you, who are gazing at you with adoration and support. You feel the strength of their gaze and their love permeates every part of your body like sunshine seeping through your veins. They give you strength and hope. Optimism flows through your body and you feel healing warmth that is life sustaining. It encompasses your mind, body, and soul.

Stay with this positive feeling and allow yourself to accept the support and love, the strength and warmth. Relax your body and feel the peace and stillness. Enjoy the circle of adoration, affection, and acceptance. Know you are worth it. You are valuable and unique just as you are."

Discussion: Explore the importance of gratitude, accepting support from others, and the significance of hope and love. Examine how using guided imagery can help create a sense of well-being and diminish stress.

MINDFULNESS: PASS THE CLAP[7]

Materials: None required.

Procedure: "Stand in a circle. One person turns to the next and makes eye contact. Clap together. That person turns around and faces the person on the other side of them, makes eye contact and they clap together, etc. Pass the clap around the circle. At some point you can change directions by sending the clap back to the person who sent it to you. And when your group is really good at sending the clap around the circle, you can pass it anywhere. This means, catch the eye of someone in the circle, doesn't have to be next to you, and clap together. They choose someone by making eye contact, and they clap together. It takes focus to know who "it" is and look at them (mindfulness of surroundings).

Then ask the group members to turn their attention to their emotions, and this time as we pass the clap, the people who just clapped take turns saying a word to describe current emotion. Next you can instruct them to focus on thoughts, urges, and body, one thing at a time (mindful of one thing in the moment)."

Discussion: "Mindfulness, being aware of the here and now, focusing on one thing in the moment, is the DBT skill reinforced through this activity. Discuss how the same activity can be performed while being mindful of different aspects, having the focus change from surroundings to emotions, thoughts, urges, body. Ask what people noticed. Ask if anyone had any urges that they didn't act on. Validate that they noticed them and allowed them to be there without taking action. Or if they did act on them talk about practicing being non-judgmental. Being aware is the first step towards making a wise choice."

THE ENVIRONMENT

Materials: Drawing paper, markers, oil pastels, and crayons.

Procedure: Share the following guided imagery[7] with group members:

The Visitor:

"As you're walking, or just sitting quietly somewhere, start to notice things as though you were a visitor to this place. As you look around you, notice sights, sounds and smells as though you had never seen, heard or smelled them before. You can imagine you are a visitor from another area or culture, or from a different species, even an alien visitor. Seeing or hearing things for the first time, from a completely different perspective. Spend a little time just looking and listening and noticing."

The Body:

"When 'Dr Who' regenerates, he immediately checks out his new body. As a newcomer or visitor, start to imagine being in your body for the first time. Notice what that feels like— what bodily sensations do you notice? How does it feel to move around, stretching those muscles, standing up or sitting down. What do those hands feel like as you move them about, stretching and wiggling those fingers, clenching those fists? As you start to walk, how is that? What do you notice about your legs—upper legs, feet and toes? Move your head around and notice what you neck and shoulders feel like. Bend, stretch and move about. What are those physical sensations? Spend a little time just noticing those bodily sensations, and imagine taking your body for its first ever walk, or any everyday activity."

The Breath:

"What would you, as a new awareness or visitor to this new body, notice about the sensations of breathing, as you breathe in, then out? Notice the sensations in the abdomen, the chest, the throat, the mouth and nose. You can notice how your attention wanders, as thoughts come in, sometimes crowding in, and your attention can follow those thoughts.

Just notice as your attention wanders, then gently bring your focus back to your breath.

Minds do wander, thoughts will come and thoughts will go, that is the nature of the human mind. As a visitor, you can stand back, notice those thoughts, feelings, sounds and sensations, and keep bringing your attention back to your breath."

Thoughts and Emotions:
"Then you can start to notice, as a visitor, the thoughts and images, feelings and emotions that come and go, in this your new body and mind. You're brand new to this body and mind, and there are no expectations for you to react to any thought, image or emotion—you can just notice them, and not respond. As a visitor, you can notice that they are just words and images, sensations, and feelings. Merely notice them as you would as a new visitor to this body and mind. Words and images, sensations and feelings: they come, and they go, and that's okay, because that's just what the human mind does."

Next ask clients to draw their impressions, feelings and/ or what they observed, e.g. an individual might draw lines and shapes to represent his reaction to the visitor imagery while another person might draw trees and clouds if he was peering out the window while listening. He might represent his bodily sensations, his breath (color, movement, etc.), wandering thoughts, emotions, sensations and /or feelings.

Discussion: "This exercise helps to develop a mindful awareness of the environment, of the body, of the breath, and of thoughts and emotions. Participants can practice the exercise as a whole, or in parts—using any part of the exercise." Creating the drawings helps individuals express their reactions and emotions, and it helps them better understand the experience of being in the moment, allowing thoughts to flow free and without judgment.

MINDFULNESS STONE

Materials: White or light-colored stones, permanent markers, brushes, magazines, glue sticks, and Mod Podge (PVA)[8].

Procedure: Group members write a saying and/or glue small pictures or words on the stone that remind them to slow down and stay in the moment. Examples may include: a photo of a rose to remind the individual to stop and smell the roses, or writing a saying such as "Take one day at a time" or "I will just focus on this moment in time." Then they paint the Mod Podge on the stone and let it dry for a few hours. This will keep the photos and words from peeling and give the stone a sheen.

Discussion: Explore the benefits of being mindful and the importance of practicing skills such as deep breathing, meditation, and non-judgmental thinking. Individuals may choose to use the stone as a paperweight to remind them to relax and not judge themselves or others.

NOTES

1. Jon Kabat-Zinn, *Mindfulness for Beginners* (2006), Audio CD (Sounds True).
2. http://franticworld.com/what-is-mindfulness/, accessed on 9 October 2014.
3. http://getselfhelp.co.uk/act.htm, accessed on 9 October 2014.
4. www.drtheresalavoie.com/userfiles/253125/file/insight_germer mindfulness.pdf (Christopher Germer, PhD), accessed on 9 October 2014.
5. www.instructables.com/id/DIY-Calming-Glitter-Jars/step6/Mesmerizing-fun/; www.doodlecraft.blogspot.com/, accessed on 9 October 2014.
6. This activity was contributed by Deborah Spiegel MT-BC, DBT informed Board Certified Music Therapist, taken from her intervention sharing blog at www.dbtmusic.com/, accessed on 9 October 2014. The procedure and discussion sections are direct quotes from her blog.
7. From www.getselfhelp.co.uk/visitor.htm, accessed on 9 October 2014. Carol Vivyan 2009.
8. ModPodge is a thin glue that can be purchased at most art supply stores including S&S and Nasco art supplies.

CHAPTER 5

Self-Awareness

With our busy schedules, it might be difficult to think about who we are, our strengths and weaknesses, our drives and personalities, our habits and values. Many people just aren't inclined to spend too much time on self-reflection. Even when personal feedback is presented to us, we're not always open to it.

Self-awareness is important for many reasons. It can improve our judgment and help identify opportunities for personal growth and professional development. Self-awareness builds self-esteem and confidence. It helps individuals decide which direction their life should be following and what their needs and desires are.

Being self-aware includes acknowledging and understanding:

- wishes and desires

- strengths

- weaknesses

- motivation or health and happiness

- challenges

- relationships with others

- barriers to achieving wishes

- beliefs and values

- self-esteem.

If an individual wants to change his life in any way, he needs to know and understand himself before he can take action. He must be aware of his desires, fears, dreams, goals, and motivations. If he is unhappy or indecisive, he must have a plan and know what has to be completed in order to head in the right direction. Until an individual recognizes his purpose, thinking patterns, and life path, he will have difficulty forging ahead and overcoming obstacles.

SELF-AWARENESS AND SELF-ESTEEM

Materials: Handouts, pencils, pens, and lined writing paper.

Procedure: Group members answer the following list of questions and discuss their answers. Emphasis is placed on listening, giving constructive feedback, and keeping an open mind:

On a scale of 1–10 how would you rate your self-esteem?

1. How did your family contribute to your self-esteem (good or bad)?

2. How did friends, classmates and/or teachers contribute to your self-esteem?

3. What have you learned to do to increase your self-esteem?

4. Which activities make you feel positive about yourself?

5. What, if anything, makes you feel good about yourself?

6. Share a few strengths and/or achievements.

7. Try to answer the question: Who are you?

8. What do you appreciate about yourself? What do you *accept* about yourself?

9. What makes you unique?

10. How would you describe yourself?

11. What, if anything, makes you feel badly about yourself?

12. What role do you play in your self-esteem, e.g. What are the silent messages you send to yourself throughout the course of the day?

13. Are you able to negotiate with yourself or others? For example: "Maybe I don't have...but I do have... Maybe I can't do this...but I can do that."

For each of the following rate yourself on a 1–10 scale:

1. Responsible

2. Trustworthy

3. Reliable

4. Honest

5. Intelligent

6. Wise

7. Kind

8. Helpful

9. Empathetic

10. Friendly

11. Likeable

12. Hard worker

13. Contributes to society

14. Creative

15. Important

Discussion: Group members share thoughts about their own self-worth. Explore how self-respect develops and is maintained, and methods to continue to increase it.

SELF-ESTEEM THOUGHTS TO PONDER

Materials: Handout, pencils, and pens.

Procedure: Clients read through the following suggestions and check the ones that they would like to utilize in their daily life:

1. It is okay to make mistakes.

2. We have the power to create and choose our life path.

3. Take tiny steps toward your goal/s.

4. Don't live for others. Live for yourself!

5. Expect change to occur at any time.

6. There is always hope.

7. "Don't sweat the small stuff." Choose your battles.

8. Take healthy risks.

9. Give yourself a pat on the back from time to time and give yourself the benefit of the doubt.

10. Spend time with people who make you feel good about yourself.

11. Accept yourself.

12. Acknowledge strengths.

13. Forgiveness helps us be free.

14. Take time to rest during the day. A short 20-minute nap is fine.

15. Exercise, mediate, practice yoga.

16. Be assertive. Learn to say, "No."

17. You may not be able to change others but you can change your reaction to them or the situation.

18. Trust yourself. Have confidence in your abilities.

19. Do you have to be right all the time? Would you rather be right or happy?

20. Don't be afraid to ask. "The squeaking wheel gets the oil."

21. Focus on the present:

> *The past is history,*
> *The future is a mystery,*
> *Today is a gift,*
> *That's why they call it* **the present!**

Discussion: Examine how the thoughts and affirmations listed below can help increase positive thinking and self-worth.

During one particular boisterous session a 50-year-old client named Joe, who was diagnosed with bipolar disorder when he was a teenager, shared that his mother never cared what he did, where he was, or whom he was with during the day or evening. He stated she was too busy working outside and/or inside the home, doing laundry, cleaning, ironing, cooking, etc. Joe believed his mother was not an alcoholic but he did see a noticeable change in her behavior when she drank. She would become increasingly withdrawn and apathetic; sometimes she seemed dazed and preoccupied. He mentioned that she never helped him with his homework and she never even asked him if he had homework. One day he came home from school with a bloody nose, black eye, and no books, and she didn't say a word. He shared that that when he was 12 or 13 years old he would hop on a train to New York City or Philadelphia with his friends and his mother never knew. He continued, "I didn't have any money but that didn't stop my friends and me from jumping over the turnstile, hopping on the train and going wherever. Once we ended up in the most dangerous neighborhood in upper Harlem." He shared another incident where he and his friends managed to make their way to Rochester, New York from Trenton, New Jersey, where they camped out for two days. When he arrived back home his mother "never noticed."

Joe remarked that his seventh grade teacher told him he would amount to nothing. She would berate him in front of the other students for being late to class or not understanding his mathematics. He shared that as a young child and teenager he felt no one cared about him. He thought it was strange that he didn't experience any consequences for his actions. He remembered wondering why his mother allowed him to "get away with murder." "I amounted to nothing, just like the teacher said, and I had a brief stay in jail for stealing from a friend's father." He also became addicted to cocaine and barbiturates.

CBT and other therapy groups proved helpful. Joe began to become aware of his self-destructive patterns of behavior and he began to understand some of the reasons he felt so negative, didn't trust others, and had low self-esteem. He has a lot of work in store for him but he says he is ready to try to transform his negative self-talk into positive self-talk. He is ready to focus on his strengths instead of his perceived weaknesses.

IDEAL SELF

Materials: Drawing paper, magazine photos, scissors, glue, markers, oil pastels, and crayons.

Procedure: Ask clients to draw and/or use magazine photos to represent the way they envisage their "ideal" self. This "perfect" self may be represented by appearance, clothes, shape, color, and attitude (facial expression), etc.

Discussion: Discussion focuses on examining the differences between one's "ideal" self and "genuine" self. Self-acceptance and exploring strengths and positive characteristics are focused upon. Methods to increase satisfaction with one's self-image are examined.

TRUE/FALSE

Materials: Drawing paper, markers, crayons, colored pencils, and oil pastels.

Procedure: Instruct participants to draw three positive things about themselves and/or their life; have them make two things true and one false. Have the other group members guess which ones are true.

Discussion: Self-awareness, socialization and communication skills are enhanced. Support participants to focus on their strengths and achievements. It seems to make it easier for participants to share achievements and positive characteristics when they do it in a playful way such as this game, otherwise modesty or embarrassment often take over and little is shared.

IDENTIFICATION

Materials: Drawing paper, markers, crayons, and pastels.

Procedure: Ask clients to fold their paper in fourths and to draw their answers to each of the following statements in the fourth:

> I am...
>
> I am not...
>
> I wish...
>
> I used to be...

Discussion: Discussion focuses on the symbols presented and the client's reactions to the sketches. Goals include self-awareness and identification of needs, hopes, and goals.

THE STORM

Materials: Drawing paper, markers, crayons, and oil pastels.

Procedure: Have group members close their eyes and imagine they are at a picnic in the forest. "All is well; it is a bright sunny day and you are enjoying the woodsy smell and delicious aroma of hot dogs, hamburgers, and steak on the grill. Your stomach is grumbling a little too loudly so you decide to take a nature walk before lunch. You enjoy observing the exquisite flowers and sniffing in their unique fragrances. The wind picks up a little but you are too entranced by the daisies and wild flowers to take notice. When your cap falls off because of a strong gust your heart skips a beat and you decide to turn back towards the picnic grounds. After a few steps the wind blows madly, the rain begins coming down in torrents, lightening and thunder make their presence known, and you think you might see a funnel in the distance. There is no obvious shelter nearby and your friends are half a mile (0.8 km) away. What do you do?"

Have clients draw what they would do next.

Discussion: Discussion focuses on the clients' choices and reactions to the emergency. Goals include problem solving and examining each individual's resourcefulness. Particular attention may be paid to the client who might give up and wait for help, and the client who immediately acts, e.g. quickly finding a low lying area to burrow into until the storm/possible tornado passes.

SELF-AWARENESS I

Materials: Writing paper, pens, and pencils.

Procedure: Direct clients to complete the following statements and then share their responses with group members:

I remember…

I realized…

I have learned…

I am pleased to think of…

I was surprised when…

I would like to remember that…

I understand that…

The thing I treasure most is…

I am good at…

I am special because…

I would like to share…

I need to remember that…

A lesson I learned was…

My wishes came true when…

As I grow older I feel…

When I was younger I felt…

The best time in my life was…

I was embarrassed when…

I felt proud when…

Discussion: Discussion focuses on the sharing of wisdom and experiences. Goals include increased self-esteem, socialization, and recollection of specific events and strengths.

ARROW COLLAGE

Materials: Construction paper, drawing paper, scissors, glue, markers, and cardboard.

Procedure: Clients cut a variety of arrows (all shapes, sizes, and colors) from construction paper. (The client can draw the arrows or the therapist may draw and cut them out beforehand if this is an issue.) At least 8 to 10 arrows per person are needed. Group participants are asked to arrange the arrows on paper or cardboard in such a way that they represent the direction of their life (e.g. are all the arrows pointing downwards or are they going in many different directions?). The arrows are then glued onto the paper or cardboard.

Discussion: Discussion focuses on exploring one's life direction, goals, and obstacles to achieving one's goals. Objectives include achieving greater self-awareness, focusing and problem solving.

SELF-AWARENESS II

Materials: Writing paper, pens, pencils, and index cards.

Procedure: Write the following questions and statements on index cards (one per card) and put the index cards in a box. Have clients each take an index card and take turns answering the questions. After a few rounds of doing this ask clients to take turns sharing one thing they learned about each group member.

Describe a typical day at home.

What is your favorite time/part of the day? What is your least favorite time/part of the day?

What are your strengths?

What are your weaknesses?

What do you need in order to be happy? What changes do you need in order to be happy? What is stopping you from achieving your goals?

What do others expect from you? What do you expect from yourself?

How do you need to improve as a person?

Who are you? What type of person are you? Describe yourself.

Describe ways you are good to yourself.

What makes you angry?

What qualities do you admire in others?

When do you feel safe?

Describe an ideal friend.

What was the nicest thing ever said about you?

What is your favorite childhood memory?

What does wisdom mean to you?

If money were no object where would you go?

Discussion: Socialization, communication and self-awareness.

FIGURE OF VALUE

Materials: Provide copies of a figure already outlined on drawing or printing paper, markers, colored pencils and crayons, pens and pencils, colored pencils, and 9 × 12 inch (22 × 30 cm) drawing paper.

Procedure: Ask participants to fill in the outline of the figure with positive words, bright colors and images, and affirmations. Examples of positive words might include: bright, creative, optimistic, smart, good mother, and cooperative and friendly.

Discussion: Discuss how the positive characteristics represented have affected one's self-esteem, attitude, and behavior. Examine strengths and achievements.

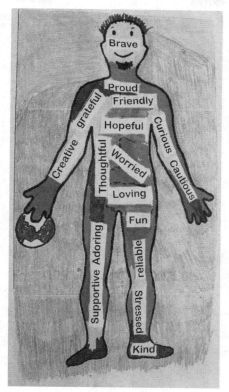

FIGURE 19

Jacob, a 51-year-old man overcoming depression and anxiety, created the outline of himself holding the world in his right hand. Jacob stated he was feeling better and starting to regain the motivation and energy he had thought he had lost forever. He chose to fill the body outline in with color first ("new happiness") and added detail to the face (a smile, his latest haircut, and a goatee). He added many positive words to the body, some of which included: "Brave, creative, grateful, proud, fun, loving, supportive, adoring, reliable, and kind." "Brave" was pasted over his nose. He mentioned he wanted it in the center of his face because he felt he was very brave to have dealt with "all my crap and to have gone through the program." Sharing that he was still recovering and realistic that every day wasn't going to be wonderful, he also added words such as cautious and worried. Jacob shared that he was holding the world to represent his improved sense of self and future goals. He stated the exercise gave him the opportunity to admire his "new qualities."

VALUES

Materials: Writing paper, drawing paper, pens, pencils, markers, and oil pastels.

Procedure: Values are the principles you hold, your standards of behavior, morals, ethics, ideas, and rules you choose to live by. When you become fully aware of your values you can choose to follow them and be true to yourself, which will in turn increase self-esteem, happiness and well-being.

Encourage participants to browse through the values listed below and add their own to the list. Then ask them to draw the three values that mean the most to them. They may use shape, design, color, and figures to represent their values.

Values:

1. loving someone

2. being true to family

3. peace

4. honesty

5. being liked

6. being appreciated

7. having peace and quiet

8. working very hard

9. being independent

10. being respected

11. being a high achiever

12. being physically fit

13. having a lot of money.

Discussion: Participants share their morals and standards for living a healthy well-adjusted life. Support them to acknowledge genuine needs and desires and those imposed by others. Examine ways to stick to one's values and follow one's own life path.

I LIKE MYSELF

Materials: Statement sheets with blanks, pens, and pencils.

Procedure: Clients complete the following statements on their sheets and then discuss their answers.

I like myself because:

- I am...

- I have...

- I can...

- I did...

- I achieved...

- I will...

- I know...

- I want to...

- I love...

- I like...

- I appreciate...

- I consider...

- I understand...

- I act...

- I had…

- I learned…

Discussion: Participants share feelings about themselves and explore ways to increase self-worth. They become more aware of attitudes, values, and behaviors by answering the questions in a spontaneous manner. There is often not enough time to filter the answers so many answers will be unplanned and genuine.

SELF-ESTEEM AWARENESS

Materials: Magazine photos, glue, scissors, construction paper, markers, crayons, and oil pastels.

Procedure: Participants are asked to think about the question, "What affects our self-esteem?" Next group members create a drawing and/or a collage that represents people, places, and things that affect their self-esteem positively. Examples may include family members, job, hobbies, accomplishments, environment, attitudes, experiences, friends, teachers, successes, etc.

Discussion: Explore ways to increase and maintain self-esteem. Encourage clients to think about situations and individuals that help raise their self-worth. Examine ways to become involved in those uplifting situations and near those enriching individuals as often as possible. Discuss the helpfulness of positive reinforcement from others, but most importantly emphasize that each individual needs to take responsibility for positive self-talk and focusing on his positive traits. One 52-year-old client emphasized, "In reality only you can decide how good a person you are."

LIFE STYLE BALANCE I

Materials: Paper plates, markers, oil pastels, crayons, pens and pencils, magazines, glue, and scissors.

Procedure: Give the participants the following instructions:

1. Outline a circle and divide it into six segments.[1]

2. In the first segment draw ways in which you work (e.g. volunteer, housework, job outside of the home).

3. In the second part draw leisure activities (e.g. music, art, gardening, etc.).

4. In the third segment draw ways in which you gain knowledge/learn (e.g. reading, watching the news, going to museums, taking trips, etc.).

5. In the fourth segment draw ways in which you socialize (join groups, call friends, etc.).

6. In the fifth segment draw ways in which you take care of your body (e.g. exercise, eat in a nutritious manner).

7. In the sixth segment draw ways in which you take care of your mind (positive self-talk, reading, crossword puzzles, spirituality, prayer, etc.).

Discussion: Encourage group members to share the importance of a balanced life style, which includes taking care of oneself physically, socially, and spiritually as well as emotionally. Examine ways participants can create a more pleasing daily schedule and environment. Emphasize the importance of taking time during the day to relax and engage in favorite hobbies and interests.

SELF-ESTEEM QUESTIONS FOR INCREASED SELF-AWARENESS

Materials: Writing paper, pens, and pencils.

Procedure: The clients rate themselves on a scale of 1–10 for each of the following:

1. intelligence

2. character (ethics, honesty, morality)

3. creativity/problem solving

4. wisdom/judgment

5. kindness/compassion

6. humor (initiating or appreciating)

7. respect/regard for others

8. self-regard

9. potential for growth, improvement, change

10. ability to learn from past mistakes

11. friendliness

12. likeability.

Discussion: Examine strengths, needs and desires, and methods to attain goals.

SHIELD OF TRAITS

Materials: Pre-drawn shield, markers, colored pencils, and pens.

Procedure: Distribute a pre-drawn shield divided into six parts to each group member. Place a rectangle under each shield.

1. In the first part, participants write their *name*.

2. In the second part they write their *strengths*.

3. In the third part they write their *achievements*.

4. In the fourth part they write their *positive affirmations*.

5. In the fifth part they write a response to: *"What I am grateful for?"*

6. In the sixth part they write a response to: *"Reasons I am worthy."*

7. In the rectangle they write *a word that is self-representative.*

Discussion: Explore strengths and positive characteristics. Review the importance of positive self-talk and optimism. Observe the unique qualities of each shield and the unique qualities of each individual. Encourage clients to embrace their distinctive characteristics.

MIND MAP[2]

Materials: Drawing paper, markers, oil pastels, pencils, and colored pencils.

Procedure: Group members are asked to create their own unique map of their mind. They may include or exclude whatever they like.

The following are general guidelines developed by Buzan (1974)[3]:

1. Start in the center with an image of the topic, using at least three colors.

2. Use images, symbols, codes, and dimensions throughout your mind map.

3. Select key words and print using upper or lower case letters.

4. Each word/image is best alone and sitting on its own line.

5. The lines should be connected, starting from the central image. The central lines are thicker, organic and thinner as they radiate out from the centre.

6. Make the lines the same length as the word/image they support.

7. Use multiple colors throughout the mind map, for visual stimulation and also to encode or group.

8. Develop your own personal style of mind mapping.

9. Use emphasis and show associations in your mind map.

10. Keep the mind map clear by using radial hierarchy, numerical order, or outlines to embrace your branches.

Discussion: Clients share thoughts, feelings, and thought patterns. They become more aware and mindful of self-talk, motivation, and attitude. Problem solving is enhanced. Mind maps may help individuals become more aware of relationship issues, connections with others and self, expression of issues, and problem solving; they help individuals organize their thoughts and priorities, and resolve conflicts.

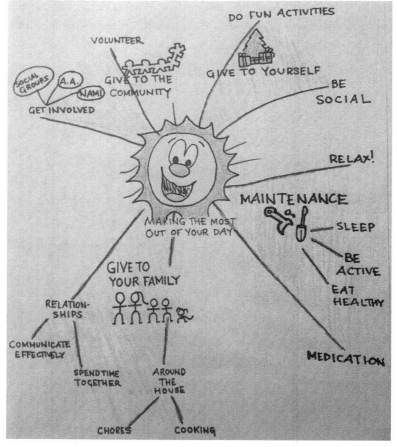

FIGURE 20

A young man in his late 20s named Jake created a personal, unique mind map. The map starts at the center, a sun, which says "make the most out of your day." Lines branch out from the sun in a variety of directions, which focus on positive ways for Jake to improve himself and his life. He added suggestions such as: do fun activities, relax, be active, communicate effectively, spend time together, give to your family, and get involved. He also added little sketches to symbolize the meaning of his ideas. He included A.A. (Alcoholics Anonymous) and NAMI (National Alliance on Mental Illness) self-help groups in his diagram. Jake designed this map in an organized manner; he used one main theme and added a variety of ways to enhance and describe the meaning of the theme. Jake shared that he is going to try to use this map to help him work on creating a more interesting and healthier life. He is focusing on being sober, thinking more positively, and not isolating.

GRATITUDE MANDALA

Materials: Drawing paper, markers, crayons, and oil pastels.

Procedure: Instruct participants to fill in the mandala with symbols and images representing things they are thankful for in their life. Suggestions may include: family, friends, love, health, sunrise and sunsets, flowers, trees, nature, rainbows, birds, puppies, babies, food, electronics, books, music, art, etc.

Discussion: Encourage clients to use the mandala as a tool that will remind them to think in a more positive manner. Explore the wonderful aspects of each individual's life, his achievements, prized possessions, loves, comforts, and interests. Discuss the simple pleasures of life, such as holding hands with a partner, watching a child laugh, or picking colorful flowers on a bright spring afternoon.

FIGURE 21

Cassandra, an attractive woman in her early 30s, remarked that she enjoyed creating this gratitude mandala. She shared that it gave her the opportunity to focus on all the wonderful people and things she has in her life, "that sometimes I completely forget about." The center of the mandala, which she thought about the longest, includes her parents, children, love (with a large red heart), and friends. She described her young children as "amazing miracles." Surrounding this center are words and concepts such as: health, music, art, birds, smile, nature, food, fun, home, trees, sunrise, and books. Christmas and religion are also included. Cassandra shared that she adores nature and watching a sunrise or sunset is a wonderful gift. She viewed this exercise as a self-esteem booster because it made her realize what a full and rich life she has. She remarked that when she feels sorry for herself she would look at the mandala to cheer herself up. She planned on framing it and hanging it in her bedroom.

SELF-ESTEEM GRID

Materials: Pre-outlined grid consisting of 20 squares measuring about 1¼ inch (3 cm) square, markers, magazines, pens, glue, and scissors.

Procedure: Group members are asked to fill in the grid with affirmations, positive words, and images that relate to feelings of happiness and high self-esteem. Examples of photos or images may include: pets, family members, symbols such as a heart, nature, flowers, etc., and/or positive words such as smart, loyal, energetic, etc.

Discussion: Clients become increasingly self-aware as they share items, thoughts, people, places, and things that contribute to joy and feelings of worthiness. They are supported to try to include these items into their life style on a more frequent basis.

It is noteworthy that many clients, even those combating depression, often find a lot of things that increase their positive feelings. Some of these items are often taken for granted (family, partners, children, abilities such as sight, touch, and taste).

FIGURE 22

This grid was designed by a 50-year-old woman named Jane who was challenged with depression and anxiety. She enjoyed the project because she was able to focus on things she enjoys and items that lift her spirits. She chose photos that represent: love (heart, family, dog), helping others (doctor helping child), flowers, exercise, and positive words such as "smile, health, community and harmony." She added the number 7 (right side of grid) to represent her lucky number. She shared that once she won $100.00 in a casino by betting on the number 7. Jane also included a woman wearing a crown, and stated she would ideally like to feel like a queen. She added strawberries to the grid because when she eats in a healthy manner she has more energy and feels inspired and motivated. The diploma represents her education and interest in learning new information. Jane stated she enjoyed placing the pictures into the boxes and wished she could slip into "little life boxes" and not be stressed. When asked which picture is most important to her, she said the woman smiling near the center of the page because she feels better when she is able to laugh and "enjoy a good joke."

NOTES

1. It is easier to divide the circle into fourths for some individuals; for lower functioning groups suggest just four segments of their life to explore. You may provide a circle already cut into four or six segments if so desired.

2. http://en.wikipedia.org/wiki/Mind_map, accessed on 9 October 2014.

3. Buzan's specific approach, and the introduction of the term "mind map" arose during a 1974 BBC TV series he hosted, called *Use Your Head*. In this show, and companion book series, Buzan promoted his conception of a radial tree, diagramming key words in a colorful, radiant, tree-like structure.

    Buzan says the idea was inspired by Alfred Korzybski's general semantics as popularized in science fiction novels, such as those of Robert A. Heinlein and A.E. van Vogt. He argues that while "traditional" outlines force readers to scan left to right and top to bottom, readers actually tend to scan the entire page in a non-linear fashion. Buzan's treatment also uses then-popular assumptions about the functions of cerebral hemispheres in order to explain the claimed increased effectiveness of mind mapping over other forms of note making.

CHAPTER 6

Self-Care

Self-care is a major component of self-esteem. Taking care of oneself physically and emotionally is a sign that you respect yourself and feel worthy. It shows that you want to live a healthy and satisfying life and are willing to make some sacrifices to do just that. It might mean eating more nourishing food such as fish, fruit, and vegetables. It might mean cutting out fats and sugar from your diet or limiting the amount of soda or alcohol you consume. It might mean trying to change bad habits such as smoking or eating too much junk food. When you feel you are "worth it" it is easier to begin a healthy regime and in turn you will most likely feel more energetic and positive.

Self-awareness plays a major role in self-care. Being aware of your negative self-talk and self-defeating attitudes is a first step towards changing them. For example, instead of thinking, "What does it matter if I don't exercise and eat pizza or hamburgers on a daily basis," an attitude of "I am going to exercise as much as possible and try to eat healthier food," can make all the difference. It can change your frame of reference and provide healthy goals. Instead of feeling sorry for yourself, which can be easier than actually working to change unpleasant circumstances, you can try to change your situation and/or environment to make it more pleasing. This may entail a move, a change of friends, or changing jobs. It might just involve a slight change of routine or a special treat for yourself such as buying weekly flowers to add some spice to your life.

Finding a purpose or goal, a reason to get up in the morning, is extremely important. It will help motivate you to work hard, stay vigorous, and maintain a feeling of well-being. Your purpose may be what you choose it to be. It can include being a parent, grandparent, friend, or teacher. It might be the desire to be a caregiver to the disabled or elderly, to take care of a pet, to volunteer your services, or to be a writer or artist. It might be to meet with friends or to go to work or school each day. A hobby or special interest might serve as a purpose. Spirituality or faith in a higher power might also serve you well.

Self-care includes being mindful and aware and communicating positively with yourself (positive self-talk) and with others. It involves socializing and surrounding yourself with positive people as much as possible. It includes being assertive (getting your needs met as much as possible) but also being flexible and finding a life style balance. Nurturing yourself and continuing to learn, experience, and grow is important. Viewing life as a process instead of a series of specific events can help individuals gain a greater perspective and may assist you to handle problems and setbacks in a healthier manner. High-quality self-care and self-awareness equal increasingly positive self-esteem.

IMPORTANCE OF SELF-CARE

Materials: Pens and pencils.

Procedure: Instruct participants to check the items on the list that they currently engage in or are interested in doing/pursuing in the future.

1. Exercise (walking, biking, swimming, etc.)

2. Nutrition (eating in a healthy manner)

3. Good hygiene (daily shower, brushing teeth, etc.)

4. Keeping your room, apartment, or house clean

5. Washing clothes, towels, etc.

6. Medical (getting appropriate tests and vaccines such as the flu shot, or mammogram if applicable)

7. Practicing good sleep hygiene

8. Socializing

9. Keeping sharp (reading, puzzles, visiting museums, etc.)

10. Positive self-talk

11. Finding a purpose (e.g. volunteering, taking care of a pet, having a hobby)

12. Allowing yourself to have fun sometimes (seeing a movie for example)

13. Treating yourself well (treat yourself as you treat others)

14. Mindfulness/meditation/guided imagery

15. Hobbies

16. The arts (drawing, painting, collage, sculpture, music, drama, and dance)

17. Keeping current (watching the news, reading the newspaper, etc.)

18. Keeping positive

19. Being assertive

20. Managing finances

21. Being a good shopper (using coupons, finding bargains, etc.)

22. Using good communication skills (e.g. using "I" statements and understanding boundaries)

23. Taking small steps (everything does not have to be done at once)

24. Asking for help when needed

25. Self-awareness: knowing your triggers and "red flags," e.g. lack of sleep, over eating, over spending, isolating, etc.

Discussion: Ask clients to share the self-care measures they checked and ways in which they'd like to continue to improve their current regimen. Discuss barriers to self-care such as lack of finances or other resources. Explore the importance of self-care and its implications for future health and happiness.

BALANCE II

Materials: Copies of a large circle with a line drawn down the center, pens, pencils, markers, and oil pastels.

Procedure: Distribute copies of the circle with the word "stress" typed in the center, or have clients write the word themselves. Suggest that participants draw and/or list things that create stress in their life on one side of the circle and draw and/or list stress-reducing techniques on the other side.

Discussion: Examine the stressors presented and explore methods to reduce them. Share techniques to lessen anxiety. For example, discuss how transforming negative thinking into positive thinking can turn negative experiences into more positive ones. Examine how clients can become more resourceful and learn to view a variety of experiences in a more optimistic and constructive manner. Discuss the importance of balance in one's life and examine methods to create a balanced life style.

HUMOR

Materials: Drawing paper, markers, oil pastels, and crayons.

Procedure: Ask clients to fold their paper in half and write the word "Funny" on one side of the page and draw something to symbolize humor and/or an amusing incident on the other side of the page.

Discussion: Discussion focuses on the importance of humor in one's life. Explore how having a good sense of humor helps you:

- stay young at heart
- cope with illness
- cope with stress
- enjoy life
- lower blood pressure
- endear people to you
- lighten burdens in difficult moments
- release endorphins
- become more spontaneous
- relax and recharge
- boost immunity
- decrease pain
- relax muscles
- prevent heart disease
- ease anxiety and fear
- improve your mood
- strengthen relationships
- diffuse conflicts
- enhance resilience
- gain/change perspective.

RECIPE FOR SELF-CARE

Materials: Recipe card outline, pencils, markers, oil pastels, and crayons.

Procedure: Provide a recipe card "Self-Care" to be filled in by group members (type the outline on a sheet of computer paper, make copies for each group member, and distribute).

Example: A Recipe for Self-Care

3 tbs. of_____

2 tsps. of_____

½ cup of_____

3 pinches of_____

1 dash of_____

1 oz. of_____

Mix all of the ingredients and apply as needed. Take one day at a time.

Discussion: Discuss the recipes and "the ingredients." Explore the ease or difficulty of the instructions and whether or not clients are following their recipes. Goals include exploration of coping techniques and objectives.

SELF-SOOTHING

Materials: Drawing paper, markers, oil pastels, crayons, pastels, pens, and pencils.

Procedure: Begin the session by discussing the value of being independent, treating oneself in a positive manner, and comforting oneself. Suggest that clients do not have to wait for others to make them joyful and fulfill their needs; they can do this on their own. For example, they can buy their own cake on their birthday or take themselves out to dinner or to a movie. Next ask clients to draw three hearts. Ask them to fill in each heart with things they do to comfort themselves.

Discussion: Discussion focuses on the size and color of the hearts and the coping skills included. Goals include raising awareness of the importance of self-care and self-nurturance.

SLEEP LIFE

Materials: Drawing paper, markers, oil pastels, and crayons.

Procedure: Suggest that clients create a design that represents their sleep life. For example, if they sleep well they may want to use shapes and colors that are gentle and soothing; if they sleep poorly, a more chaotic design might be representative.

Discussion: Discussion focuses on the way in which the drawings represent one's sleep patterns. Explore the benefits of a sound sleep:

- improved memory
- better mood
- less depression
- increased healing
- more energy
- longer life span
- reduces stress
- healthier heart
- healthier diet/lower calorie intake
- strengthens immune system
- more alert—decreases accidents of all types.

Goals include exploring methods to improve sleep and focusing on the role sleep plays in reducing depression, anxiety, and stress.

WORRY STONES

Materials: Nontoxic clay, Sculpey (can be bought in most art supply stores or purchased online), polymer clay (this clay is not powdery or dusty and remains workable until baked; it can be baked in the home oven), index cards, plastic knife, and tray.

Procedure: Have group members choose three different colors and cut small pieces of clay for them (three marble-sized pieces) or have clay ready beforehand. Ask clients to squish the colors together and twist the clay a few times. Have them create a sphere and place it on the index card. Ask clients to choose a thumb and press it down into the clay until the bottom is flattened. Ask them to etch their initials into the bottom of the clay gently and place the clay back on the index card. Clients can take the clay home and bake it themselves or the leader can bake the pieces and distribute them back to clients.

Discussion: Discussion focuses on the stones' *healing qualities* and the importance of keeping a positive outlook. Self-soothing, calming techniques are explored. Having a tangible object that can be used for healing is very therapeutic.

RELAXING AT HOME

Materials: Pen and paper.

Procedure: Create a list of activities that can be done at home to ease stress. This can be created by the group leader and/or with the clients. The leader makes a copy of this list and distributes it to clients. Group members check off the items that appeal to them. Next clients are asked to draw the activity that they find most helpful, and present it (temporarily) to the person sitting next to them. Have that person discuss how the activity could help him relax, and how he feels about receiving it.

Discussion: Clients share ways to relax at home. Goals include sharing and exploration of coping skills.

Examples include:

- taking a warm shower or bath
- watching television
- listening to the radio
- listening to a guided imagery CD
- doing a puzzle
- engaging in a hobby
- reading
- exercising
- working on a craft
- drawing
- baking
- journaling
- scrap booking
- playing a computer game
- meditating/being mindful
- knitting/needlepoint
- sitting on one's front porch, terrace or deck, or peering out of a window and people watching.

SHOPPING CART

Materials: Drawing paper, markers, pens, pencils, magazines, glue, and scissors.

Procedure: Provide an outline of a shopping cart (trolley) or have clients draw one.[1] Outlines of shopping carts may be found on Google Images if desired. Ask participants to fill in the cart with self-care items, e.g. food, shampoo, mouthwash, lotion, books, puzzles, CDs, laundry detergent, vitamins, etc. Magazine photos may be used if desired and pasted into or near the cart.

Discussion: Explore the items placed in the cart and their importance in the clients' lives. Goals include examining various ways to take care of oneself physically and emotionally.

FIGURE 23

Zandra, a very talkative woman in her early 40s, filled her shopping cart with "many necessities." She stated that she enjoys shopping and always feels good after she has filled the refrigerator and stocked the cabinets with food. She also remarked that some months she doesn't have enough money to do so because her husband spends too much money on "his items," which may include "cigarettes, cigars, fast-food, beer, and lottery cards." Zandra stated that she becomes enraged when he is irresponsible and self focused because the whole family suffers. She remarked that she hates it when her children do not have their basic needs met, which include healthy food to eat and milk to drink each day.

Zandra includes her three children in the cart because they "are my world and go everywhere with me." She adds flowers, a heart to represent love, blueberries for health, ice cream, friends, vacation, art, play, sleep, waffles, a coffee cup, music notes, and electronics. Vacation was added as a future goal. Zandra mentioned that she placed art in the cart because she enjoys being creative, especially with her children. They often read, bake, draw, and play with clay. She shared that she needs love and family in her life more than anything else. She remarked that she could live for days without food and a few days without water, but if her family didn't love her she couldn't live at all.

DECREASING STRESS

Materials: Drawing and writing paper, pens, pencils, markers, and pastels.

Procedure: Have clients share a variety of stress management techniques and then provide a list for them (see below). Discuss the methods with clients and then have group members draw themselves engaging in one of the techniques discussed.

Self-care techniques:

- take mini breaks throughout the day.

- practice acceptance (like yourself)

- talk rationally to yourself

- get organized

- exercise

- focus on the "here and now"

- talk to friends

- watch habits (eat well, get enough sleep)

- meditate

- Practice breathing exercises

- take one day and one task at a time

- be creative (draw, write, journal, do crafts, etc.)

- volunteer/help others

- reach out to friends and family for support

- read/watch a funny movie or television show

- keep learning (for example, a new language)

- keep active (go out to dinner, to plays, museums)

- take your medication and see a doctor regularly.

Discussion: Discussion focuses on the artwork and methods to utilize the self-care techniques presented. Goals include stress reduction, compilation of a repertoire of coping mechanisms, and decreasing stress.

WELL-BEING

Materials: Magazines, construction and drawing paper, scissors, glue, and markers.

Procedure: Direct group members to create a collage with magazine photos, cut paper, and/or drawings of people engaged in healthy behaviors (exercising, cycle riding, brushing teeth, etc.).

Discussion: Discussion focuses on the significance of the photos/ artwork chosen, the placement of the images on the paper, and their meaning for the client. Goals include supporting a healthy life style and self-care.

AMUSING COLLAGE

Materials: Magazines, drawing paper, glue, scissors, and markers.

Procedure: Ask clients to search for photos that they find uplifting, amusing, entertaining, and enjoyable. Instruct them to glue the photos on the page in order to create a pleasing arrangement.

Discussion: Have group members share their work and point out pictures that interest them. Encourage clients to keep the collage on display at home to brighten their mood. Explore the benefits of keeping positive, smiling, and making time for leisure activities and enjoyment.

DIET AND NUTRITION

Materials: Drawing paper, writing paper, pens, pencils, and markers.

Procedure: Discuss the importance of good nutrition with clients. Examine how healthy eating habits affect mood and behavior as well as physical health. Explore the benefits of eating fruits and vegetables as well as whole grains, fish, and lean meats. Next suggest that clients draw or list the types of food they tend to eat and ask them to describe the effect the food seems to have on their behavior. For example, for some individuals drinking alcohol makes them anxious and causes sleep disturbances.

Discussion: Discussion focuses on the connection between the foods we eat and mood, energy, anxiety, depression, and recovery. Goals include education and awareness about the importance of good nutrition for emotional and physical health.

SELF-CARE EXPLORATION

Materials: Writing paper, pens, and pencils.

Procedure: Ask group members all or some of the following questions for greater self-awareness. They may write their answers or share verbally.

- What area of self-care do you need to improve?
- How are you taking care of your health?
- How healthy is your diet? What types of food do you eat?
- Do you cook?
- Are you exercising?
- Are you keeping your house, apartment or room tidy?
- What has your "self-talk" been like lately?
- How are you reducing stress?
- How well do you sleep at night?
- How can you try to keep yourself alert when you feel groggy during the day?
- How can you approach people when you want to make a friend or form a new relationship?
- What "vice" would you like to give up?
- What are your strengths?
- What do you do in your spare time?
- What do you need that you don't have? How can you get it?
- How are your finances? Do you budget your money?
- Are you medication compliant?
- How are you "nurturing" yourself?

- Are you reading? Do you journal?
- What or who are you thankful for?
- What is your purpose? Do you have a goal?

Discussion: Clients explore methods to take better care of themselves physically and emotionally. Examine how high quality self-care improves attitude, mood, and behavior. Generally, self-esteem increases when individuals practice a healthy life style.

ENERGY COLLAGE

Materials: Drawing paper, markers, oil pastels, magazine photos, scissors, and glue.

Procedure: Find and/or draw pictures of activities and behaviors that increase energy, e.g. someone swimming, cycling, exercising, laughing, etc.

Discussion: Observe movement and vitality in the artwork and explore methods to increase motivation and vigor. Examine individual energy levels and discuss how energy affects one's mood, attitude, behavior, and activity level.

HEALING

Materials: Magazine photos, drawing paper, markers, oil pastels, glue, scissors, and crayons.

Procedure: Ask group members to think about the following question, "What do you need in order to heal?" Instruct clients to find photos and/or draw pictures of people, places, and things in their life they need to feel better physically and psychologically. Examples may include a partner, a new home, a better attitude, friends, medicine, hope, love, etc.

Discussion: Explore methods to raise self-worth and hope for the future. Examine ways to self-soothe and heal oneself.

Discuss possible reasons for procrastination and staying stuck in a rut, and emphasize that each individual has the power to begin his own healing process.

VISUAL JOURNALING

"Visual journaling is a creative way to express and record life's experiences, feelings, emotional reactions, and our inner world—visually and verbally. Essentially, visual journaling can become a potential key to the art making process. By committing to the visual journaling process, one can learn how to access his inner language of imagery and express it both visually and verbally, while exploring the connection between image and world."[1]

Materials: Journal or sketchbook, paints, assorted brushes, ink, markers, pastels, pens, pencils, cut paper, collage materials, magazine photos, stamps and pads, glue, and scissors.

Procedure: Clients are asked to begin keeping a creative journal of their daily mood, experiences, and thoughts. They may use a variety of materials, images, doodles, and textures to represent their feelings. Words and affirmations may be included. Pictures may be layered and overlapping of words and images is encouraged. Individuals may enter one entry a day or multiple entries, depending on their mood and motivation.

Discussion: Participants are encouraged to explore their journal entries if they feel comfortable sharing with group members. They will be supported to share insights and symbolism. Patterns of thinking and behavior will be examined. Clients will be encouraged to think of their journals as ongoing works in progress where they can gain insight into their "emotional and cognitive experiences."

CREATIVE SELF-CARE BULLETIN BOARD

Materials: Bulletin board or large square of cork, push pins, drawing paper, scissors, magazine photos, and markers.

Procedure: Participants are provided with square pieces of cork or inexpensive bulletin boards. They begin to decorate them, adding photos, words, affirmations, drawings, etc. that focus on self-care. They may update their boards daily or weekly.

Discussion: Explore the variety of decorative methods that may be used to create a feeling of hope and optimism. Discuss the importance of focusing on positive affirmations to increase self-worth daily. The boards will be a reminder of strengths and unique traits.

LIFE BALANCE

Materials: Drawing paper, markers, oil pastels, pens, magazines, scissors, and glue.

Procedure: Encourage participants to create a self-care mandala. Group members may write, draw and/or use photos. The following lists can be used as a reference to aid in the exploration of self-care.

Physical wellness:

- getting enough sleep

- eating well

- exercising (reduces stress, helps heart/blood pressure, helps guard against osteoporosis, increases serotonin (feel good chemical in brain), lowers depression, and increases self-esteem)

- visiting the doctor and getting appropriate tests

- drinking moderately or not at all

- not smoking

- not drinking too much coffee or soda

- being well groomed

- taking the stairs instead of the elevator

- parking far away and walking
- making an exercise schedule
- dancing
- stretching
- engaging in sports
- trying yoga

Nutrition: (affects mood, energy level, weight, and self-esteem)

- eating small meals throughout the day so you don't get too hungry
- drinking water instead of sugary drinks
- eating breakfast
- limiting processed carbohydrates (e.g. wheat instead of white bread)
- eating more vegetables, fruit, chicken and fish
- eating at least 5–7 servings of fruit and vegetables each day
- not eating 2–3 hours before bed
- Trying small energy boosters such as peanut butter on crackers or celery
- other healthy snacks include: hummus and rice cakes or pita chips, or egg whites on wheat toast

Spiritual wellness:

- searching for meaning in our life
- spirituality doesn't have to focus on religion—it can be the belief in a higher power or nature, family, music, art— you decide
- it is something to believe in that gives you a purpose, hope and/or inspiration

Stress reduction:

- meditation
- mindfulness—being in the moment
- deep breathing
- prayer
- positive self-talk
- exercise
- yoga
- creativity/art
- dance/movement
- poetry/creative writing

Creativity and self-expression:

- journaling
- gratitude list
- creative writing
- poetry
- art
- dance
- music/movement
- sculpture/woodworking

Leisure activities:

- always take time to relax during the day, even if it is just a few minutes (perhaps take an extra long shower or luxurious bubble bath, or spend a few minutes reading a favorite book or magazine)

- play and enjoy yourself
- keep that inner child alive and active
- read, draw, dance, do puzzles
- visit museums, travel, attend plays and concerts
- socialize; invite friends for coffee, lunch, or dinner
- go bowling, watch a baseball games, or join a club
- surf the Internet and learn something new

Affirmations and positive self-talk:
Find affirmations that appeal to you and keep them handy for future reference. Hang a few on your refrigerator. Examples of positive affirmations include:

- Take one day at a time.
- Do the best you can and then leave yourself alone.
- Accept what you can't change.
- Avoid people who cause you stress.
- Be assertive.
- Change what you can, but don't dwell on what you can't.
- Think positively.
- "Feel it, process it, and let it go."
- No one can make you feel inferior without your consent.

Discussion: There are many aspects involved in self-care. Some of theses aspects include: Physical, spiritual, emotional, intellectual, environmental, financial and social.

Wellness is a balance of all of these factors—a feeling of well-being. Explore ways individuals can increase life satisfaction and health.

MY HANDS

Materials: Drawing paper, markers, pencils, colored pencils, and pens.

Procedure: Outline both hands and fill them in with "what they have done over the years." Then check off the following and/or your own ideas.

My hands have:

1. washed dishes

2. cleaned clothes

3. dusted

4. washed floors

5. made lunches

6. cooked dinners

7. changed diapers

8. baked

9. knitted/crocheted

10. earned money

11. patted children's heads and backs

12. played games

13. soothed others

14. worked with tools

15. hammered nails into walls

16. been clenched in a fist

17. clenched with worry

18. created art

19. made a mess

20. cleaned up messes

21. hugged family members and/or friends

22. yearned to hug family members

23. rowed a boat

24. built something

25. driven a car

26. bathed my children

27. planted flowers

28. mowed the lawn

29. clapped

30. snapped

31. worked with clay

32. been adorned with rings and jewelry

33. caught fireflies or small animals

34. petted an animal

35. waved hello or goodbye

36. made the thumbs up sign in agreement or for a job well done

37. designed jewelry.

Discussion: Explore experiences, strengths, and relationships. Discuss how one's hands may be reflective of one's abilities and motivation and can serve as a reminder of one's history.

CREATIVE STRESS REDUCTION

Materials: Drawing paper, writing paper, pens, pencils, and markers.

Procedure: Encourage group members to relax through creative expression, which may include: journaling, poetry, drawing, mandala work, etc.

Suggestions include:

1. Write a poem, short story, or journal.

2. Create a picture utilizing adult coloring outlines.

3. Design your own drawing or mandala (circle used for focusing and healing, and stress reduction).

4. Work on needlepoint/hook rug project.

5. Make a gratitude list and illustrate it.

6. List goals and methods to attain them.

7. Draw a peaceful, safe place.

8. Draw your stress (include shapes and colors).

9. Experiment with line, color, shape, and design.

10. Fill in lovely flower outline.

11. Close your eyes and think of a pleasant memory. After a few minutes open your eyes and draw the memory or part of it.

12. Write a letter to your stress.

13. Collage work.

14. Visual journaling.

Discussion: Creative work helps increase self-esteem and reduces anxiety. It helps individuals focus, and provides a purpose and an enjoyable activity. It is inherently beneficial and can also serve as a distraction from stress and worry. Anxiety and anger may be released in a healthy and appropriate manner and can be better contained if so desired. Engaging in creative work allows the individual the time to process problems and come up with possible solutions.

INCREASING SELF-WORTH

Materials: Four circles printed on a sheet of paper, drawing paper, markers, colored pencils, and pens.

Procedure: Instruct participants to draw four circles on the page (or distribute circles already printed). Inside each circle they should draw and/or find one or more photos that represent:

1. productivity (e.g. working onside or outside the home)

2. leisure time activities/hobbies

3. social connections

4. acts of kindness (volunteering/supporting others).

Discussion: Assisting others and engaging in activities helps individuals feel healthier and provides them with a purpose. They focus their attention on people, places, and events as opposed to concentrating on their own internal stressors. Individuals become stronger physically and psychologically, and increasingly motivated. Helping others often improves mood and attitude and assists in stress reduction and the enhancement of concentration and focus.

NOTES

1. Michael Bell, celebrity artist: http://pintangle.com/2009/11/29/the-visual-journals-of-michael-bell/, accessed on 9 October 2014.

CHAPTER 7

Reflective Writing

Creative writing, journaling, and poetry provide us the opportunity to share feelings and experiences in a very personal and artistic manner. We are in control as we put our thoughts and dreams on paper. We are in charge of what we write and how we write; we can be truthful or fanciful if we wish. Experiences that are too painful to share verbally can be written and shared only if we choose to do so. We can hide our notes and refer to them as we feel comfortable. Creative writing allows us to reach out to others in a non-threatening manner. It permits us to communicate our feelings and gain a more realistic perspective. After expressing troubling thoughts we can view our feelings from a distance and not "own them" so much. We can gain more perspective and analyze our work at our leisure. Being a writer gives us the opportunity to identify, recognize, and process our feelings. Poetry, for instance, becomes a vehicle for sharing happiness, sadness, fear, frustration, love, and hope. It can lift our spirits and free the mind. Self-awareness and self-esteem are enhanced. Creating poetry can help us when we are stuck; it allows us to gain more freedom as we learn to think more abstractly. Journaling allows us to keep a diary of our experiences and associated thoughts. It can be considered a written reflection of achievements, questions, fears, and day-to-day activities.

Writing "gradually eases pain and strengthens the immune system."[1] Some studies show that it helps to relieve stress and depression, and may heal illnesses such as arthritis, asthma, and even cancer. Creative writing assists us with interpersonal conflicts and problems. It enables us to organize our thoughts, relive pleasant memories, and remember achievements. It allows for self-exploration, insight, and reflection. Creative writing is a healing art that helps reconcile conflicts, express emotions, and share beliefs and values. It is relaxing, stress reducing, and enjoyable. It helps keep us young and our memory, thinking, and focusing sharp.

POSITIVE FEELINGS

Materials: Writing paper, pens, and pencils.

Procedure: Participants are asked to work together to create a group poem or story that represents positive, uplifting feelings or themes. They may decide to work together from the start or divide into groups for a while and then meet after about 15 minutes to discuss their progress. One individual may take charge or everyone could have equal say; group members will decide how to proceed. A secretary to take notes and write the completed poem may be useful.

Discussion: Participants decide who will read the poem aloud. They will share their thoughts and reactions to it. Suggest they discuss ways in which they relate to the poem and parts of it they find meaningful. Discuss the value of working as a team and the feelings of camaraderie elicited. The following is an example of a poem created by a group.

Positive Feelings
Happy, good, smiling faces,
Helping others,
Helping ourselves.
Doing our best,
Making mistakes.
Its okay,
Being real,
Being human,
Letting ourselves just be.
This is how,
We can feel free!

BRAIN DUMPING[2]

Materials: Pens, pencils, and writing paper.

Procedure: "Brain dumping is a specific form of free writing in which you can just write out everything that is on your mind. You sit down at your computer or grab a pen and do not stop writing until you feel like it's time to stop. You can set a timer or a page requirement, but it's best to let your mind tell you when you're done. When you perform your brain dump, you literally do not stop. Just keep moving at a quick rate to try to keep up with your thoughts. You can start with a specific thing that is causing you stress or anxiety, but let your mind take you wherever it wants to roam. The point is to get all your thoughts out on paper so they don't eat away at your mind. This is a good way to gain a new perspective of your situation with a deeper level of understanding about how you feel. It's also a great way to release your creativity and free your mind to think of ways to get out problems. This process helps weed out destructive or unproductive thoughts, to get the thoughts that will help you move forward."

Clients are asked to begin writing anything on their mind and not to stop until they feel they have nothing else to share. If they stop too quickly the group leader may need to suggest they work "a little longer."

Discussion: Participants share insights and/or portions of their writing if they are comfortable doing so. Discuss the benefits of this exercise and whether or not clients were able to free their mind in order to express a variety of thoughts and feelings. Explore if some of the contents shared had been forgotten or repressed before clients engaged in this exercise. Was anything unexpected expressed? Did clients feel a sense of freedom and/or release?

WORD LIST PASS AND MANDALA

Materials: Pencils, pens, drawing paper, markers, oil pastels, crayons, and colored pencils.

Procedure: This exercise may need two sessions if there is a time constraint or if clients/leaders feel there are too many steps to follow. Ask clients to sign their name at the bottom of their sheet of paper. In this way they know which paper they began working on first. Instruct them to write a positive word or brief phrase on the paper and then ask them to pass their paper to the person sitting to their right (wait a few minutes before asking them to pass their paper so they have time to reflect). Now everyone has a second sheet of paper and they write another positive word on this sheet of paper, and again they pass the paper to the person on their right. This keeps happening until everyone has written a positive word on everyone else's paper and the clients receive their original sheet back. They will know it is theirs because they will see their name written on the bottom of the page. Each client should now have a sheet filled with positive words and statements. Next have them outline a circle from a paper plate on a sheet of drawing paper in order to create a mandala. Suggest they create a design within the mandala that reflects feelings associated with the positive words. For example, a mandala that focuses on words like cheerful, friendly, and fun might be filled with colorful shapes, movement, wavy designs, or smiling faces, suns, flowers, etc.

Discussion: Discussion focuses on the word lists and the composition of the mandala. Goals include being positive and exploration of attitude, mood, and perspectives on life.

ATTRIBUTES

Materials: Envelopes, pens, pencils, writing paper, markers, oil pastels, and colored pencils.

Procedure: Provide each client with an envelope and several small slips of paper. Each group member writes his name on the envelope, decorates it, and then writes an attribute about the person sitting next to him. The attribute is then placed in the envelope. The process is repeated as the envelopes are passed around the room from one individual to another. The exercise is over when everyone has written a comment for everyone else in the group. When the envelopes are full they are given to the leader who selects one of the envelopes and chooses a comment to read out. The person whom the comment was written about will try to guess the name of the person who wrote it. At the end of the exercise each person may keep his envelope as a reminder of his positive qualities.

Discussion: Goals include increase of self-esteem and confidence. Questions to ponder include:

- How do you feel after hearing the supportive statements?
- When was the last time you received a compliment (before today)?
- What is the benefit of hearing and giving support?
- Were you able to accept the support?
- What will you do with your envelope?

SELF-ESTEEM WARM-UP

Materials: Writing paper, pens and pencils.

Procedure: Ask clients to write as many positive things about themselves as they can in five minutes.

Discussion: Discussion focuses on sharing positive attributes. Goals include increased self-awareness and acknowledgement of strengths.

SELF-ESTEEM CIRCLE

Materials: Pre-drawn circle with 6–12 petal-like projections emanating from it (openings should be large enough to include one sentence), markers, pens, and pencils.

Procedure: Direct clients to write something positive about themselves in the center of the design. In the other areas have them list accomplishments (even minor ones).

Discussion: Clients share accomplishments, awards, and achievements. Goals include increased self-esteem and acknowledgement of positive work and experiences.

COMMUNICATION SKILLS

Materials: Writing paper, drawing paper, pens, pencils, markers, oil pastels, and crayons.

Procedure: Suggest to group members: "Share a time that your words healed someone else. What did you say? How did it feel to be supportive?" Next ask clients to list at least five words that may be used to encourage others, and then draw a picture, write a poem, or write a description symbolizing the feeling/s gained from helping another person to feel better.

Discussion: Clients share their positive experiences and strengths. They discuss what it feels like to be the helper in a relationship. The importance of one's words, actions and attitude is explored. Goals include increased self-worth, assessing positive qualities, exploring new goals, and volunteer opportunities. Clients are often awakened to the possibilities of helping others; they begin to see how they can be a powerful force in others' lives.

HAPPINESS II

Materials: Writing paper, drawing paper, pens, pencils, and markers.

Procedure: Images may be drawn or found on Google Images or other sites on the Internet. Ask clients to write a list of things that make them happy. Compare the lists among group members;

look for similarities and differences. Next ask clients to draw a time (recently or in the past) they felt joyful. Discuss the drawings, focusing on specific people, circumstances and/or environment. Discuss methods of attaining the happiness that was represented in the drawings. Examine each group member's present level of happiness. Ask clients to score their happiness on a 1–10 scale where 10 is feeling the most happy and 1 is the least happy. Suggest the group members compose a list of ways to increase joy. Some examples are:

- finding fulfilling hobbies
- volunteering
- joining a group or club (to make a friend)
- accepting yourself for who you are
- being kind to yourself
- *carpe diem* (living for the day, being mindful, taking time to smell the roses.)

Discussion: Discussion will focus on what happiness means to each individual and various methods to attain contentment in life will be explored.

POSITIVE TRAITS

Materials: Drawing paper, markers, and colored pencils.

Procedure: Instruct group members to write a positive characteristic about themselves using each letter of the alphabet (they have the option of skipping a few difficult letters such as x and z). The letters may be pre-written so clients will find the instruction easier to follow. When this is completed ask clients to create an illustration using the letter that represents their most outstanding quality. They may decorate the letter and in addition represent the quality they described. For example, if the letter C stood for creativity, a design might include a colorfully decorated C and a palette drawn next to it. If the letter H stood for humorous, the person may draw the letter H using lots of colors and add a picture of a smiling face next to it.

Discussion: Clients share strengths and talents. They identify abilities and focus on positive attributes.

SUPPORT

Materials: Writing paper, pencils, and pens.

Procedure: Have clients share various instances where they helped others. Ask them how they felt and how they think the other person/s felt at the time. Discuss the fact that roles may change during various stages of our life; we are allowed to ask for help. We do not always have to be the caregivers. Suggest clients speak about ways in which they need support now (for example, help doing laundry, car rides, assistance with grocery shopping, cooking, needing extra warmth, attention and love, etc.). Next ask participants to divide their paper in half and write ways they could gain support from others on one side of the paper and ways they could feel positive about taking the support on the other side of the paper. Examples might include:

- *Support:* arranging not to be alone, asking children and friends to visit more often

- *To feel positive:* bake family and/or friends a cake; tell them how much you admire them

- *Support:* going to a support group or senior center

- *To feel positive:* give helpful advice to others, bring cookies or other treats

- *Support:* moving to an independent living community where life is made simpler or find a roommate to share the rent and housekeeping

- *To feel positive:* create new relationships, share interests with others, volunteer your services

- *Support:* asking friends and/or neighbors to drive you to the supermarket or help carry your bags into your house

- *To feel positive:* make them a cup of tea, help them if possible when they are in need, be there to listen to them when they need advice or desire to vent feelings.

Discussion: Discussion focuses on the conflict between being the *helper* and *helpee*. Goals include acceptance, increasing self-esteem, and focusing on ways to get needs met in a healthy manner.

WHO AM I?

Materials: Writing paper, pens, and pencils.

Procedure: Suggest that clients write a paragraph answering the question, "Who Am I?" After they write their paragraph ask them to draw a self-portrait in any way they wish. Emphasize that an abstraction (line, shape, color) is perfectly acceptable.

Discussion: Discussion focuses on the descriptions (ask clients to read them aloud) and the associated representations. Goals include self-awareness and identification of strengths and weaknesses. It is important for clients to view themselves in a variety of roles (mother, friend, teacher, helper, sister, etc.), and not just as a client or someone who has depression or bipolar disorder, for example.

FIGURE 24

Meg, a 64-year-old woman suffering from bipolar disorder, drew this self-portrait. Meg tends to experience extreme paranoia and always believes the government is searching for her in order to torture her and ultimately to kill her. Meg has been practicing self-help measures such as deep breathing, meditation, positive thinking, and distraction so that she can function and live in an independent manner. Meg's portrait looks the way she might have looked 30 years ago. She still has blonde hair but it is bleached; her present-day face is lined and looks well worn. Her own body is ever so slightly humped as if she is holding the weight of the world on her shoulders. In this drawing she is represented as an engaging, young, spry woman, standing to attention with a lovely smile on her face. Her hands are placed behind her back as if to hide something; what's her secret?

Meg liked this rendering and smiled when her peers shared that they saw the similarity between her and the woman depicted. Meg remarked that she wished she was young again because in the past she had friends and her family was with her: "Now they rarely see me; they can't be bothered." When asked what the woman might be thinking about, Meg shared that the woman is wishing that her family will visit and that she will meet a handsome man.

FIGURE 25

Concetta, a 29-year-old woman diagnosed with schizophrenia, drew a large, colorful heart to represent her personality. She seemed very focused on her artwork and would not stop drawing even after group formally ended. She remarked that she loved the bright colors and shared, "Each color is the love I feel towards the universe." She seemed extremely pleased when group members complimented her artwork (usually she compliments her own artwork). While she was drawing she shouted out various words and phrases such as "love," "I want a boyfriend," "Send all the Columbians home," and "All young women from different countries are pretty." She had been very concerned with her appearance and the appearance of others, especially young women.

In response to the question, "Who am I?" she wrote: "My name is Concetta. When I was a little girl my first language was Spanish, but as I grew up in Newark, New Jersey, it converted into English. I am an extremely nice person with a big heart. My biggest pet peeve is when people are jealous, because due to this I have my problems. A lot of people are jealous of me because I am pretty. Then they are nasty to me and that's why I don't have friends. People don't understand me and it's very hard. I feel emotions and

I am different from most people. I love the lord with all my heart along with my family and friends."

It is noteworthy that this client appeared focused and clear while drawing, but she seemed unfocused and exhibited hallucinatory behavior during the group discussion, and at the beginning and end of the session. Engaging in a creative pursuit helped her relax, reduce anxiety, and focus.

ACROSTIC POEMS

Materials: Paper and pencils.

Procedure: An acrostic poem uses the letters of a word for the beginning of each line of the poem. The poems do not need to rhyme.

Example: **CAT**

C: Chloe sat under a tree

A: And the sky was bright blue

T: Two birds chirping a lovely song.

Ask clients to think of a simple word and write a poem using that word as the outline.

Discussion: Discussion focuses on the poem and symbolism within it. Goals include creative expression, focusing, and sharing of ideas and feelings.

Client Examples:

Home:
Home is where the heart is,
It is filled with plants, love and
colorful flowers,
My plants grow beautifully,
Every one of them is amazing.

Bill:
Back some twenty years ago,
I took a wrong turn in the road,
Leaving the familiar path,
Later I saw my mistake and
returned.

THE LITTLE ENGINE THAT COULD

Materials: Writing paper, pencils, and pens.

Procedure: Clients take turns reading the book *The Little Engine that Could*[3] aloud or group leader reads it. When the story is finished ask clients to share their thoughts and reactions to the story. Next ask them to write a brief essay about a time when they needed extra strength to achieve a goal.

Discussion: Ask clients to read their stories. Then suggest group members explore one or more of the following questions:

- What is the moral of the story?

- Which of the engines/trains can you best relate to?

- How do you "push" to move ahead?

- Has there been a time in your life you had difficulty "pushing"?

- What is the difference for you between the phrases "I think I can" and "I can?"

- Describe what it means when you use the words "I can't."

- Is there a difference between "I can't" and "I choose not to"?

- What changes in your life can be made by shifting your thinking from "I can't" to "I can"?

- What are the benefits of "standing still" (in other words staying the way you are and not changing)?

- What changes would you like to see in your life in the near future? What changes would you like to see in the more distant future?

- How can you achieve these changes?

LIFE STYLE BALANCE II

Materials: Writing paper, pens, and pencils.

Procedure: Discuss ways clients take care of themselves (e.g. meditation, aerobics, eating healthily, etc.). Next have them write a brief story about an individual who chose to nurture himself after a period of self-neglect. Inform clients that the story could be imaginary or based on reality.

Discussion: Discussion focuses on the narrative and the significance of it. Ask participants if they relate to the main character in the story. Goals include greater self-awareness and identification of self-care techniques.

LOVE YOURSELF

Materials: Writing paper, pens, and pencils.

Procedure: Read the following poem, "Always Love and Accept Yourself" to group members. Explore the clients' associations to it. Next ask participants to list the ways they demonstrate love and respect for themselves.

"Always Love and Accept Yourself"
Author Unknown

I accept myself completely.
I accept my strengths and my weaknesses,
My gifts and my shortcomings,
My good points and my faults.
I accept myself completely as a human being.
I accept that I am here to learn and grow,
and I accept that I am learning and growing.
I accept the personality I've developed,
and I accept my power to heal and change.
I accept myself without condition or reservation.
I accept that the core of my being is goodness
and that my essence is love,

and I accept that I sometimes forget that.
I accept myself completely, and in this acceptance
I find an ever-deepening inner strength.
From this place of strength, I accept my life fully
and I am open to the lessons it offers me today.
I accept that within my mind is both fear and love,
and I accept my power to choose
which I will experience as real.
I recognize that I experience only the results
of my own choices.
I accept the times that I choose fear
as a part of my learning and healing process,
and I accept that I have the potential and power
in any moment to choose love instead.
I accept mistakes as a part of growth,
so I am always willing to forgive myself
and give myself another chance.
I accept that my life is my expression of my thought,
And I commit myself to aligning my thoughts,
more and more each day with the Thought of Love.
I accept that I am an expression of this love.
Love's hands and voice and heart on earth.
I accept my own life as a blessing and a gift.
My heart is open to receive, and I am deeply grateful.
May I always share the gifts that I receive
Fully, freely and with joy.

Discussion: Goals include focusing on self-care and strengths, increasing self-esteem, and positive thinking.

IN THE MOMENT[4]

Materials: Writing paper, pens, pencils, drawing paper, markers, crayons, and oil pastels.

Procedure: Ask clients to complete the phrase: "Right now I feel…" Suggest they write at least three statements reflecting how they feel at the present moment. Next ask them to draw one or all of the feelings represented in any way they please.

Discussion: Discussion focuses on the written descriptions and associated artwork. Goals include identifying and expressing current feelings and increased self-awareness.

LOVE LETTER

Materials: Pens, pencils, envelopes, writing paper, markers, and crayons.

Procedure: Suggest group members write love letters to themselves. Encourage them to add a lot of self-praise and support. Next suggest they decorate the letter and envelope to reflect the positive words included in the letter.

Discussion: Discussion focuses on the importance of having self-worth, "being present (being aware of ourselves)," and self-acceptance. Goals include increasing self-esteem and confidence.

THE BUTTERFLY EFFECT[5]

The Butterfly Effect: "Chaotic processes, such as the weather can be affected by small changes in initial conditions, so that the flapping of a butterfly's wings in Tahiti can, in theory, produce a tornado in Kansas."

Materials: Writing paper, pens, and pencils.

Procedure: Read the brief story: "The Young Man and the Starfish: A Motivational Story About making a Difference."[6] Explore the meaning and clients' reactions to the story. Next suggest that group members write about a time/s that they made a difference in someone's life. Emphasize that it does not have to be a great feat; it can be a favor, a show of empathy or affection, a suggestion, or support.

Discussion: Discuss the Butterfly Effect. Emphasize how one person can make a huge impact on the life of others. Explore that everyone, regardless of age, has a lot to share, give, and teach. Examine ways in which clients have helped others in the past and can be of help in the future. Goals include increased self-esteem and motivation to volunteer, interact with others, and become more active.

GRATITUDE II

Materials: Drawing paper, markers, and pens.

Procedure: Read the following poem and discuss the meaning. Suggest group members draw and/or write ways in which they are thankful. Examples might include illustrations of their family, a sun, trees, flowers to represent nature, etc. They may write about being healthy, having a home to live in, friends, lovely memories, etc. Life's battles and lessons learned may be examined.

Be Thankful: A Short Poem
by Author Unknown

Be thankful that you don't already
have everything you desire.
If you did, what would there be to look forward to?
Be thankful when you don't know something,
for it gives you the opportunity to learn.
Be thankful for the difficult times.
During those times you grow.
Be thankful for your limitations,
because they give you opportunities for improvement.
Be thankful for each new challenge,
because it will build your strength and character.
Be thankful for your mistakes.

They will teach you valuable lessons.
Be thankful when you're tired and weary,
because it means you've made a difference.
It's easy to be thankful for the good things.
A life of rich fulfillment comes to those who
are also thankful for the setbacks.
Gratitude can turn a negative into a positive.
Find a way to be thankful for your troubles,
and they can become your blessings.

Discussion: Clients share their "riches" and things that are enjoyable in their life. They may explore how problems and challenges have enriched their life in various ways. Goals include exploring coping skills and methods to optimize happiness in their lives.

A client named Miss Helen, challenged with a myriad of physical problems and bipolar disorder, wrote this brief poem for me. It was her last day in the program and she wanted to say goodbye in her own unique manner.

Last Day
By Miss H

My last day here and I am sad,
You'd think I would be very glad.
Your words of hope and genuine style,
I'll think of you often all the while.
Therapy or art, you're the best by far,
They are your forte without a mar.
So lovely a smile, encouragement abound,
You speak of the positive wherever it is found.
You're a "gem in the ocean," so they say,
I'll miss you Miss Susan, that's surely everyday.
Thank you again for all you say.
You "light up my life" in every way.
Love,
H.

BEAUTY

Materials: Writing paper, pens, and pencils.

Procedure: Group members work together to list everything they find beautiful in life. Next they create a poem from the word list. They may add additional words and phrases if they please. The poem doesn't have to rhyme or be within any specific format. It will be personal and unique.

Examples of words that might be used include: sun, flowers, roses, raindrops, rainbow, gold, children, glitter, sunset, smile, blue sky, diamonds, mountains, babbling brook, etc.

Discussion: Clients share their poems and their associations to them. Goals include: working together (teamwork), socialization, problem solving, creative thinking, and looking at the positive aspects of life.

ABOUT ME

Materials: Drawing paper, pen, pencils, markers, oil pastels, and crayons.

Procedure: Instruct clients to read the following questions. Suggest they fold their paper into thirds and illustrate their answers to three of the questions. The remaining questions may be explored later on in the session.

1. What time do you get up in the morning and what time do you go to sleep?

2. What are your favorite movies and/or television shows?

3. What do you like to eat?

4. What type of music do you like?

5. What characteristics do you admire in others?

6. What are your strengths?

7. Do you have pets?

8. What are your future goals?

9. Who comprises your family?

10. Where do you live?

11. Where were your born and where did you grow up?

12. Where/what is your favorite place?

13. Where would you like to go on vacation?

14. What were you like as a child?

15. What games and/or sports have you played in the past?

16. Who do you like?

17. Who do you admire?

18. Who puts a smile on your face?

19. If you were on a deserted island what three items would you bring?

20. What do others tend to say about you?

Discussion: Goals include socialization, sharing, and self-awareness.

SHARED INFORMATION

Materials: Writing paper, pens, and pencils.

Procedure: Instruct clients to write a brief description of themselves consisting of at least three facts on a sheet of paper. Have them crumple their paper and place it in the center of the table. The group facilitator mixes the papers up and clients choose one of the crumpled papers. Everyone gets a chance to read from the paper they chose while other group members guess who wrote the narrative.

Discussion: Goals include sharing, increased communication, unity, and learning about others. This is a pleasant game and serves as an effective icebreaker.

EXPRESSIVE VERSE

Materials: Writing paper, pen, and pencils.

Procedure: Participants are asked to create a poem *of sorts* that reflects their feelings as it "tells their story." Emphasize that the poem can be written in any way they choose (as a short story, Cinquain, limerick, etc.). Rhyming is optional.

Discussion: Self-esteem often increases when individuals express true emotions and share inner thoughts. Everyone has a story to tell and sharing it in a creative manner may be a cathartic experience for clients. It allows them to uncover core beliefs and helps them develop coping skills by analyzing behaviors and attitudes described in the poems, and then working on a plan of action. Below are a few examples of expressive work written by group members:

Positive Feelings
Happy, good, smiling faces,
Helping others,
Helping ourselves.
Doing our best,
Making mistakes.
It's okay,
Being real,
Being human,
Letting ourselves just be.
This is how
We can feel free!

Ode to a Smoker
By Miss H

I smoke a Camel every day,
Rain or shine or come what may.
For me it's really such a treat,
For others this is not too neat.
It doesn't help C.O.P.D.
But I am speaking just for me.
I get a high with every puff,
To give it up is really tough.
A smoker I have been for years,
To give it up I fight back tears.
I love it so it means to me,
A reality check it's time you'll see.
To beg for a cigarette a daily chore,
These friends of mine couldn't ask for more.
They give and give to all in need,
At break time is when you sow the seed,
Of needing help just one more time,
To ask and ask not too sublime.
Sometimes a beggar more than not,
It's time for all too really take stock.
Am sorry to start at age 33,
Never thought these Camels would conquer me!
It's Sunday now I'm on my own,
The seeds of which have already been sewn.
I'm sure to smoke sometime today,
But deep in my mind it's not okay.
I smoke you Camel without a thought,
Satisfaction is what is really sought.
A vicious cycle it is yours to see,
A pattern of wanting - not helping me.
So "thank you" for listening what I say is so right,
And to those who are smoking, you know of my plight,

Camels I smoke I can't always find,
To make matters worse it's the strongest of kind.
So here's to the smokers, for it's not just mine,
This issue is major, we'll learn in good time.

The woman who wrote this verse was very pleased with her work and her self-esteem greatly increased as she shared her poem with others. She is in her late 60s, challenged with bipolar disorder and has severe breathing and other health issues, but she keeps smoking. She knows she is a victim of her habit and hopes to have the willpower to quit one day soon. Unfortunately, at this point in her life she views smoking as a gift to herself and it is the one thing she looks forward to every day. The goal would be to find an equally satisfactory way of enhancing happiness and the sense of peace she derives from cigarettes.

The following poem was written by a client in his 40s challenged with schizophrenia. He often has difficulty articulating his thoughts but he is able to draw and express deep personal feelings through his beautiful poetry. It is his way of reaching out to others when even saying "Good Morning" is often a chore.

In the quest to survive,
A token sense of esteem,
Here we revive,
Our wayward aims and dreams,
Here we epitomize,
To What this reality seems,
Here we personify,
Our wayward aims and dreams.
To the sage a simple trust,
That perfection never exists,
In the throws of our lust,
Here we persist,
In this lies a must,
In this tandem we insist.
Here a spirit is defined,

A power greater than all,
In what we choose to leave behind,
In Hell or Heaven's hall,
If we choose to believe,
The greatest manifestation of fate,
If we can conceive,
Of the powers that destroy and create.

The following poem was written by a young man in his 20s who suffered from depression and low self-esteem. His girlfriend recently ended their year-long relationship, which increased his powerlessness and low self-regard. He remarked that writing this poem helped him feel better about himself and allowed "his expression to come through."

Losing you, I lost my mind.
Bad things happen, I cannot lie,
But if I could those things would change,
My love, my feelings, they're still the same.
I told you once my love was you,
And till this day that love is true.
You are my heart, no need to lie,
You're the tear from heaven's eye.

POSITIVE PHOTOS

Materials: Each participant receives a few pages filled with photos of people who appear bright, strong, and productive, e.g. someone gardening, smiling, taking care of a child, driving, etc. These photos may be from magazines or copied from Google Images.

Procedure: Clients are asked to place a check next to the photos they can relate to in some way. For example, perhaps they presently feel strong, like a body builder or a construction worker, or perhaps they have felt strong in the past. Lastly they are asked to write a few lines about the photos selected and the way in which the photos remind them of their own positive characteristics and experiences.

Discussion: Clients share instances where they were productive and helpful to others. They are supported to focus on their strengths, achievements, and abilities.

MY NAME

Materials: Writing paper, pen, and pencils.

Procedure: Participants write their name vertically on a sheet of paper. Next to each letter of their name they are asked to write a positive attribute.

Example: **SAM**

    S: Stunning

    A: Amazing

    M: Masterful

Next ask clients to elaborate with specific examples, e.g. "I was *stunning* in that red dress. I was *amazing* when I carried 15 pounds of cement, and I was *masterful* when I aced the chemistry test."

Discussion: Acknowledge and explore positive characteristics and achievements. Using their name helps individuals *own* their strengths.

POSITIVES IN A BAG

Materials: Drawing paper, markers, pens, and pencils.

Procedure: Participants draw or receive an outline of a shopping bag. They are asked to write anything they could think of to keep in the bag that will help them stay positive. Examples include: children, smiles, the sun, treats, flowers, rainbow, affirmations such as "take one day at a time," exercise, meditation DVDs, positive self-talk, and photos of family members, etc.

Discussion: Participants share techniques to keep positive and to increase self-worth. They are encouraged to keep adding to the bag on a daily basis.

PRESCRIPTION FOR HAPPINESS

Materials: Writing paper, pen, and pencils.

Procedure: Participants are asked to write a prescription for happiness, e.g. exercise each day, smile a lot, eat in a healthy manner, try to make friends, practice good sleep hygiene, focus on strengths, be grateful, etc.

Discussion: Clients share their prescriptions and they also share whether or not they are following their own orders. Ask group members if they want to add to their prescriptions and/or follow someone else's prescription. Explore what they are *not doing*, what they *need to continue to do*, and what they need to *begin to do* to feel better and improve their life.

FUTURE GOALS

Materials: Pens, pencils, and lined writing paper.

Procedure: Clients write about future plans and goals. They are asked to include a description of their desired life style including relationships with family and friends.

Discussion: Writing helps individuals clarify and target goals. It enables them to visualize what they want to do, and where they want to be in days, weeks, or years to come. It provides the opportunity to examine methods to achieve ambitions and it encourages hope and excitement about future possibilities. People often gain self-awareness and increased self-esteem, as well as an increased feeling of control when they write. Solutions to various problems may be explored simultaneously with goal exploration.

When an individual writes, he is in charge; he is the master of what happens. He becomes the master of his fate.

Encourage participants to share whether or not their expectations and desires are realistic. Explore ways to achieve goals and explore methods to break down barriers standing in their way. Examine strengths that will help clients pursue their life purpose.

SELF-TALK

Materials: Lined writing paper, pens, and pencils.

Procedure: Create two columns on a sheet of paper by drawing a line down the middle of the sheet. One side of the paper will have the heading "Negative self-talk" and the other side will have the heading "Positive self-talk." Under negative self-talk have participants write all the unconstructive things they say to themselves during the course of the day. For example: "I am stupid, I can't do it, I am not as worthy as him." Under positive self-talk support them to list the constructive things they would like to think to themselves. These could include: "I am smart, I did a very good job, and I like myself." Support participants to add to the lists on an ongoing basis.

Discussion: Participants are asked to write a brief summary of how they feel when they examine the negative self-talk and how they feel when they review the positive self-talk. Explore the importance of their healthy and unhealthy dialogue. Ask clients to share the last time they supported themselves for a job well done. Review the importance of their thoughts when trying to increase self-esteem and optimism.

NOTES

1. Woolston, (2000) http://consumer.healthday.com/encyclopedia/depression-12/depression-news-176/writing-away-trauma-644988.html.
2. Condensed from Matt Maresca, www.pickthebrain.com/blog/building-self-esteem-with-writing-therapy/.
3. *The Little Engine That Could*, (1930), Watty Piper.
4. Modified according to a suggestion by John Fox, CPT.
5. www.aps.org/publications/apsnews/200406/butterfly-effect.cfm, accessed on 9 October 2014.
6. www.mastermason.com/brothergene/wisdom/starfish_author_unknown.htm, accessed on 9 October 2014.

CHAPTER 8

Diverse Directives

Self-esteem is a gift that we can bestow upon ourselves. Determination and practice are important components of self-esteem. As children our self-worth comes mainly from family, teachers, and friends, but as adults we can begin to take control of our thoughts, reactions, and emotions regardless of our environment and experiences. It is not an easy task but by practicing various techniques, engaging in positive self-talk, and by becoming increasingly self aware we can make significant changes in our thinking and way of life.

When our self-esteem improves our relationships are usually better, we are more assertive, and we become satisfied with who we are; we don't have to change for others.

The exercises in this chapter encompass an array of techniques aimed at enhancing self-esteem. Included is a potpourri of exercises ranging from mazes, vision boards, and collage work to the design of affirmation cards, which aim to decrease anxiety and increase positive feelings and acknowledgment of strengths.

It would be beneficial to browse through the exercises and choose a few to explore daily or periodically. They aid with self-awareness, the development of insight and eventual healing. Some of the techniques will take a few minutes to do while others might take a few days. It is up to each person to decide how much effort he wants to expend. In general the more someone practices the techniques presented the quicker he will learn new skills and be able to apply them to a variety of situations.

INCREASING FEELINGS OF SELF-WORTH

Materials: Paper, pen, pencils, and copies at the 30 item list below.

Procedure: Clients list a variety of ways to help increase self-esteem. In addition, they are asked to include ways their self-esteem has been positively impacted in the past.

Discussion: Participants share ideas and provide examples from their own experiences. Then the following suggestions listed below are read aloud by group members and explored. Participants may be asked to check (tick off) the ideas they have or are planning to use in the future.

1. Focus on achievements; include even minor achievements such as learning to ride a bicycle or learning to swim.

2. Focus on what is positive in your life.

3. Make lemonade out of lemons; look at the positive aspects of life as opposed to the negative.

4. Accept yourself. This doesn't mean you can't have goals or improve aspects of your personality and life. It means trying to be content with the "real you." It means changing for yourself and not to please others.

5. Associate with positive people.

6. Don't compare yourself to others.

7. Have a safe, comfortable place in your home just for you, even if it is a corner of a room.

8. Forgive yourself and let go of guilt.

9. Allow yourself to make mistakes; you are only human.

10. Remember you choose how to respond and react to problematic people and situations.

11. Take tiny steps so you won't be overwhelmed.

12. Help others, volunteer.

13. Exercise; increase your endorphins and sense of well-being.

14. Meditate.

15. Don't take yourself so seriously all the time; develop your sense of humor.

16. Accept compliments; say "Thank you."

17. Create a gratitude list.

18. Live your own life, not the life others want you to live.

19. Make your own decisions; you can't please everyone.

20. Be assertive.

21. Learn a new skill.

22. Stop negative self-talk.

23. Take healthy risks.

24. Don't compare yourself to others.

25. Remember you are the one who decides your self-worth.

26. Avoid exaggerations, especially when the exaggerations are negative. Stay away from words like "always, never."

27. Accept imperfections; you are only human and everyone makes mistakes.

28. Don't bully yourself.

29. Replace self-criticism with support and encouragement.

30. Focus on what you can do instead of what you can't do.

BRAG BOOK

Materials: Construction paper, drawing paper, manila folders, markers, crayons, oil pastels, collage materials (such as glitter, wool, buttons, and sequins), scissors, glue, and magazines.

Procedure: The manila folder will contain the book. Place about three or four sheets of construction or drawing paper within the folder and use a three-hole punch to create holes in the folder. Have clients create a cover for their book by drawing images and designs on the outside cover of the folder using markers and the collage materials. They may label the folder "Brag Book" or anything else they desire. Next have them create a decorative frame around the remaining inner pages using marker, pastels, and collage materials. The pages will be attached using ribbon or wool and tied in knots or bows. Have clients fill in the brag book with words, reminisces, photos, and illustrations of family members, friends, and themselves.

Discussion: Have clients share positive thoughts, relationships, and experiences. Goals include increased self-esteem and a focus on gratitude and positive aspects of their life.

LIFE BOX[1]

Materials: A tissue or cigar box, or similar type of cardboard box; magazines, construction paper, collage materials such as buttons, felt, sequins, and glitter; glue, scissors, marker pens, and small pieces of white paper.

Procedure: Have clients decorate the outside of the box so that it represents them in some way. They may use the magazine photos and/or the collage materials. Have them find pictures that are self-representative and place them in the box. They may use their own photos if desired. They may also write about themselves and family members and place those descriptions inside the box. When the boxes are complete they will share the boxes and photos with group members. This project may take two or three sessions.

Discussion: Clients share their history, experiences, relationships, interactions with family members, and facts about themselves. Goals include self-expression, life review, sharing, increased communication with others, and increased self-esteem.

SERENITY POEM DECORATION[2]

Materials: "Serenity Prayer" poem or other self-help poetry (provide at least one or two additional poems), markers, oil pastels, crayons, glue, and scissors.

Procedure: Distribute the poem to clients on 8½ × 11 inch (21 × 28 cm) paper and have them glue it on a sheet of 12 × 18 inch (30 × 45 cm) paper. Suggest clients create a design/environment surrounding the poem that reflects its meaning. Clients may use another poem if they don't choose to use the Serenity Prayer. In addition, they may change the prayer by omitting "God" and beginning instead with "Grant."

Serenity Prayer
By Reinhold Niebuhr

God grant me the serenity
to accept the things
I cannot change,
the courage to change the things I can,
and the wisdom to know the difference.

Discussion: Group members share symbols and colors in their artwork that represent their thoughts and feelings about the poem. Goals include exploration of coping skills, self-awareness, and mindfulness.

THINKING POSITIVELY

Materials: Writing paper, drawing paper, markers, pens, and pencils.

Procedure: Discuss what it means to think in a positive manner. Explore the meaning of optimism (hopefulness, brightness, cheerfulness). Ask group members to draw a quick sketch representing hope or optimism. Next have clients write and/or verbally share their answers to the following questions.

1. Are you more of an optimist than a pessimist?

2. When you make a mistake can you forgive yourself? Are you able to forgive others?

3. What type of things do you do to make yourself happy?

4. When you are in a new situation how do you feel?

5. Do you socialize with others?

6. Do you look forward to getting up in the morning and starting the day?

7. On a scale of 1–10 (where 10 is the most hopeful and 1 is the least hopeful) what number are you in terms of hope for a brighter future?

8. Describe some positive things about yourself.

9. What makes you smile?

10. When was the last time you felt joyful?

11. When was the last time you laughed?

12. When was the last time you told someone how special they were?

13. When was the last time someone told you how special you are?

Discussion: Clients explore the symbols represented in their artwork, their approach to life and their responses to the specific questions. Goals include examination of attitude, mood, and self-talk.

IMPROVING RELATIONSHIPS I

Relationships are a very important part of well-being and self-esteem. Almost everyone needs someone to care about, someone with whom they can share life's ups and downs, and someone who will be there in times of need. Supportive friends, family, and partners raise feelings of worthiness and can provide individuals with a purpose for "being." They can provide the impetus to take healthy risks and to recover from illness and injury. Isolation and/or unhealthy relationships can create stress, anger, frustration, and very low self-esteem. They can be depleting and debilitating; therefore understanding how to form relationships and keep them strong is a crucial part of good self-care.

Materials: Paper and pencils.

Procedure: Clients discuss positive or problematic relationships they are presently encountering. Next they list methods to better handle the turbulent relationships. They also list suggestions to keep the positive relationships healthy. General tips to improve relationships are then read aloud by clients and shared.

Discussion: Explore the following questions:

- What qualities do you look for in a friend?

- What qualities do you bring to a friendship?

- Describe an "ideal" friendship.

- Which communication skills would you like to improve in order to make and maintain friends?

- Was it easier to find friendship in the past or is it easier now?

Tips:

1. Listen carefully. Everyone wants to be validated. Maintain good eye contact and let the other person know you understand what he is saying even if you disagree.

2. Be clear. Think before you speak.

3. Try not to verbally attack the other person. Be assertive, not aggressive.

4. Show gratitude and appreciation.

5. Compliment when it is deserved.

6. Compromise.

7. Choose your battles.

8. Be flexible.

9. Forgive as much as possible.

10. Keep expectations realistic.

11. Be supportive.

12. Show interest.

13. Empathize.

14. Be genuine.

15. Share with friends or partner.

16. Give your friend or partner the benefit of the doubt.

17. When you express anger watch your manner, body language, and tone of voice. Don't threaten (your friend may take you up on it).

HAPPINESS III

Materials: Paper and pencils.

Procedure: Group members share what happiness means to them. Ask them what they need in their life to increase feelings of well-being and self-worth. Explore what period in their life made them the most joyful. Ask participants to create a list of ways they can improve their present circumstances and lift their spirits. Lastly, provide the following list and read and explore the suggestions with group members.

Discussion: Discuss how the following suggestions can positively impact clients' lives. Examine which suggestions are feasible and which might be difficult to pursue and why:

1. Meditate.

2. Exercise.

3. Volunteer.

4. Eat nutritious foods.

5. Get sufficient sleep.

6. Socialize more often.

7. Draw, paint, and be creative.

8. Move; dance to music.

9. Don't worry what others think—be yourself.

10. Take time to relax during the day.

11. Engage in positive self-talk.

12. Find a purpose.

13. Learn something new.

14. Laugh a lot.

15. Don't take yourself too seriously.

16. Allow yourself to play and enjoy life.

17. Make a gratitude list.

18. Appreciate what you have; don't dwell on what you don't have.

19. Focus on what's in your control.

20. "Do your best and then leave yourself alone."

21. "Feel it, process it, and let it go."

22. Try new things—take healthy risks.

23. View problems as challenges.

24. Create goals for yourself.

25. Take tiny steps toward change.

26. Take one day at a time.

27. Replace negative thoughts with positive ones.

28. Choose your battles.

29. Give yourself frequent pats on the back.

30. Be mindful—live in the present.

31. Let go of past guilt.

32. Try to become better organized.

33. Treat yourself as you treat others.

34. Focus on positive traits.

35. Think about accomplishments.

36. Keep a journal of feelings.

37. Listen to guided imagery.

38. Accept that there will always be change in life.

39. Understand that life is a process—a journey.

40. Avoid negative people.

41. Learn to say no. "Saying no to others is saying yes to yourself."

42. You do not have to be perfect.

43. Redefine success.

LEISURE AND SELF-ESTEEM

Hobbies and leisure activities help individuals learn more about themselves and assist in developing skills such as creativity, abstract thinking, drawing, writing, and improvement of coordination and memory. Engaging in hobbies gives us the opportunity to do something special and to focus on our strengths and capabilities. Pursuing interests allows us to learn, grow, and expand our repertoire of friends, abilities, and talents. We may realize potential in an area we never imagined such as painting, science, language, or music. Our self-esteem is raised as we challenge ourselves and find success in new endeavors, which are enjoyable and fulfilling. Leisure activities may serve as our "purpose," a reason to get up in the morning, and/or a reason to socialize with others and remain an integral part of society.

Materials: Handouts, pens, pencils, and lined writing paper.

Procedure: Clients fold their paper in half. On one side of the page they list hobbies and interests they presently engage in and on the other side they list hobbies and interests they would like to engage in, in the future.

Discussion: Clients share interests and ways in which their feelings of self-worth are raised while engaging in positive pursuits.

SELF-ESTEEM DRAWING PASS

Materials: 9 × 12 inch (22 × 30 cm) drawing paper, markers, crayons, pens, and pencils.

Procedure: Each participant is given a sheet of drawing paper and chooses one color marker or crayon. Clients may only use that one color throughout the exercise. They are asked to write their first name at the bottom of the paper (their name is written only on this first sheet). Next clients write an affirmation, positive word, or statement, (or they may sketch a positive image on the paper), keeping in mind that everyone will have a turn writing/drawing on each page. After a few minutes the leader says "pass" and the paper is passed to the person sitting to the right. This pattern of writing/drawing positive affirmations keeps occurring until each participant receives his original paper back. When the original paper is returned it should be filled with affirmations and images.

Discussion: Participants share their artwork and explore positive images and statements. The specific colors used will help identify group member's contributions. Methods to enhance feelings of self-worth and happiness will be explored and connection with others is a primary goal.

ACHIEVEMENTS I

Materials: Lined paper, pens, and pencils.

Procedure: Clients create a list of their past successes. Have them include as many achievements as they can think of including small ones like making a new friend or cleaning their house. Next have them place a strength they needed to use in order to accomplish the goal in parentheses next to the achievement, e.g. finding a new job (perseverance) or learning to swim (bravery).

Discussion: Explore capabilities and positive characteristics. Encourage participants to use their strengths to function more effectively at work, home, and in social situations.

SUPPORT

Materials: Pens, pencils, and copies of an outline of a person filling the entire 9 × 12 inch (22 × 30 cm) sheet of paper.[3]

Procedure: Outlines can be found on Google Images if desired. Group members are each given a piece of paper with a figure outline. They are asked to fill in the figure with the names of people in their life who they find supportive and comforting now and/or in the past. If they choose to do so, participants may also add the names of people who play a role in their life but are not so understanding.

Discussion: Individuals generally feel better about themselves when they surround themselves with positive, supportive people. Individuals who provide encouragement, acceptance, and praise elicit feelings of worthiness and increased life satisfaction. Many people are motivated to grow and take healthy risks when they know they have caring people in their life. Clients may explore which individuals help them feel confident and which individuals create an atmosphere of negativity. It is wise to try to focus on the people who are helpful and lessen or eliminate connections with those who are hurtful and/or disparaging.

Filling in the figure provides an outline that adds extra insight. Examine where the names are placed and the significance of the placement for the client. For example, is the name placed in the head, heart, or stomach? If it is placed near the heart does it mean that the person is dear? If the name is placed on the foot does it mean that person is someone the client would like to kick? Questions such as, "Who can the outlined figure represent?" may be explored.

AFFIRMATION CARDS

Materials: Index cards, markers, pens, pencils, glue, scissors, and lists of affirmations.

Procedure: Participants are given a list of about 30 positive affirmations (e.g. take one day at a time, I am worthy, etc.). The type should be small enough for the statement to fit on an index card. Each client is then given five index cards. They are asked to write their own affirmation, or cut and glue an affirmation from one of the statements on the list and place it on the index card. Participants keep doing this until they have five cards with five different affirmations. Once completed, the group leader gathers all the cards, shuffles them and then re-distributes them so that everyone receives five new affirmation cards.

Discussion: Group members take turns reading and assessing the affirmations. Towards the end of the session they may keep their affirmation cards or trade with others. They are encouraged to repeat the affirmations at least once a day in order to think more positively.

Clients greatly enjoyed this project. They were able to share their associations to the affirmations and their positive thoughts. Participants gave examples of how they used the affirmations to help them feel better and how the affirmations related to their beliefs and improved attitudes. One woman said she only chose affirmations that were generic because she wasn't ready to say anything positive about herself. Another woman said she liked *"Every day is a new beginning,"* because *"it is wonderful to think you can begin a new each day with a fresh start."* Yet another woman liked *"Feeling less sensitive about what others think"* because she constantly worried about what others felt about her, and she thought she was constantly being judged. Someone complained, "if your childhood is bad, it is very difficult to have good self-esteem." This individual was able to begin to understand that as an adult she has the power to choose how to feel about herself. Many of the older patients liked *"today I will feel gratitude and count my blessings."* They said they feel positive when they thank the heavens for waking up to one more day and being alive. One client felt good about the fact that "everyone was comfortable enough (nine people in group) to share their thoughts and positive statements, and allow others to remain where they were with their feelings."

BUILDING SELF-CONFIDENCE

Materials: Pens, pencils, markers, writing, and drawing paper.

Procedure: The procedure is divided into two parts; two sessions may be needed.

Part 1:

1. Ask clients to describe their level of self-confidence.

2. Have them create a personal self-esteem graph using weeks, months, years, and/or decades to mark levels of self-esteem. The graph may be created using a plain line with markers indicating self-esteem levels or it may be as unique as the client likes.

3. Explore the following: When was self-esteem the highest? When was it the lowest? Describe significant highs and lows. Is the graph smooth, bumpy, etc.?

Part 2:

1. Instruct participants to list factors that affect their self-esteem.

2. Ask participants to create a list of things they can do to raise their self-confidence.

Discussion: After participants have created their lists ask them to share their thoughts with their peers. Introduce some of the following ideas if they have not been shared by the participants. Suggest that group members keep an ongoing list and add to it whenever an idea strikes them as helpful.

1. Focus on past successes (no matter how small).

2. Think in a more positive manner (transform the negative into the positive).

3. Take healthy risks (e.g. applying for a new job).

4. Practice self-acceptance.

5. Accept that "It's enough to do my best."

6. Let go of guilt (guilt keeps you stuck).

7. Don't label yourself or others (we are complicated people and "wear many hats").

8. You are just as good, if not better, than others.

9. See the "good" in yourself.

10. Focus on your strengths.

11. Find positive people to socialize with.

12. Develop a support system.

13. Learn new skills.

14. Take time to be mindful.

15. Volunteer.

16. Join social groups.

17. Engage in hobbies.

18. Try to be organized.

19. Don't give up (remember the famous swimmer, Diana Nyad).

20. Avoid people who are negative.

21. Keep affirmations where you can see them and say a few aloud each day.

22. Keep a gratitude list.

23. Keep an achievement list (of every little achievement such as making new friends or learning a new skill).

24. Smile/laugh as much as possible.

25. Try to see the humor in life.

26. Don't worry what others think.

27. Focus on people and things you love.

28. Exercise.

29. Focus on the positive aspects of your life.

30. Accept who you are.

31. Develop a sense of humor.

32. Make a list of your positive qualities.

33. Be true to yourself. Live your own life—not the life others have decided is best for you.

SHARED ATTRIBUTES

Materials: Pens, pencils, markers, writing paper, glue, scissors, index cards, and drawing paper.

Procedure: The leader gives each client an index card with the name of one of the group members. Clients are asked to write a positive quality about that person on the card. Next clients give the card back to the person whose name is on it. Clients now glue their card on a sheet of construction paper, and then draw and/or find a magazine picture to represent their special quality.

Discussion: Discussion focuses on the attributes chosen for each individual, the client's reaction to his attribute, and the picture/drawing that depicts it. Goals include connecting with others and identifying positive characteristics.

HUGS

Materials: Writing paper, pens, and pencils.

Procedure: Ask clients to give imaginary hugs to each other by saying, "I hug you because…" completing the statement. Have each individual share until everyone receives a hug. After all group members are hugged have clients write down or draw their reactions to being hugged or to giving a hug.

Discussion: Discussion focuses on giving and receiving support. Goals include increasing self-esteem and gaining a greater awareness of strengths and positive characteristics. This project works particularly well when a group member is very upset. In such a case each client supports the one individual as he receives all of the group's love and comfort. In a recent therapy session a male patient felt unloved, undeserving, and "less than a man." He was tearful and extremely depressed. The support from his fellow group members helped him feel less isolated and needed; he felt part of the community. Although he wasn't at the stage in his recovery where he actually believed all of the compliments he received he was able to find some comfort in the warmth and friendship bestowed upon him. It helped him open up and share some of his issues, which include being abused as a child and discounted by his mother: "You are worthless," she said as she spat on him. This was an example of the verbal abuse he shared with the group members. At the end of the session he walked out of the room with his peers surrounding him and guiding him. They were able to replace symbolically the affection he didn't receive from his own parents. Although temporary, the support probably helped him avoid an inpatient hospital stay.

BEING POSITIVE

Materials: Writing paper, drawing paper, pencils, colored pencils, markers, oil pastels, and crayons.

Procedure: Help clients create a list of positive images such as flowers, rainbows, a sun, sunsets, babies, smiling people, families, vacation spots, nature, etc. Next suggest clients choose one or more of the images and illustrate them.

Discussion: Explore the positive imagery and the feelings elicited. Goals focus on the benefits of having an optimistic attitude.
Benefits of being positive:

- increased life span (some studies show an increase of approximately seven years)
- lower rates of depression
- better mood and outlook
- lower stress levels
- greater resistance to certain illnesses (especially colds)
- reduced death from cardiovascular disease
- better coping skills
- better performance at work and play
- more successful relationships
- broader perspective on life.

AFFIRMATION MAGNETS[3]

Materials: Drawing paper, colored pencils, pencils, markers or permanent markers if available, magnet backing, and magnetic write on/wipe off strips or magnetic circles.

Procedure: Review various affirmations and distribute a list to clients. Suggest they choose an affirmation that appeals to them. Have clients write the affirmation on the drawing paper and create a design next to or surrounding it. Ask them to repeat the same sketch on the magnet. It is helpful to first experiment on the drawing paper since it is difficult to change words/illustrations once marker is used on the magnetic surface. Suggest that the magnet be placed on their refrigerator or other surface that can be viewed daily.

Sample affirmations:

- Loving myself heals my life. I nourish my mind, body, and soul.

- My body heals quickly and easily.

- I know that I deserve love and accept it now.

- I attract only healthy relationships.

- I am my own unique self—special, creative, and wonderful.

- I am at peace.

- I pay attention to everything around me and I am careful and deliberate with each of my movements. I am graceful and mindful.

- All things happen for a purpose. My past experiences also had purpose. I have learned from my past and am now free from it. I choose to release the past and live in the now.

- I accept and love myself.

- This too shall pass.

Discussion: Discuss the affirmation list and the chosen affirmations. Review the positive impact that the words and phrases can have on one's mood and attitude. Goals include increased self-esteem and awareness of the power of self-processing and self-talk.

SUPPORT IN A BOX

Materials: Tissue, cigar box, or white cigar shaped box,[4] glue, scissors, construction paper, magazines, tissue paper, a variety of collage materials such as buttons and sequins, small strips of paper, pens, and pencils.

Procedure: Decorate the box using magazines photos, positive words, colorful shapes, and other collage materials. Then cut out about five to ten small strips of white paper (or leader distributes the strips already cut out). Have clients write positive statements and affirmations on each slip of paper and place the slips in their boxes. Suggest they keep their boxes at home and read the affirmations when they feel anxious and/or depressed.

Discussion: Discussion focuses on the box designs and the positive statements placed in them. Goals include self-acceptance and exploration of coping techniques to self-soothe.

SELF-ESTEEM MAZE

Materials: A maze for each client, markers, pens, and pencils. Clients may design their own maze if they prefer.

Procedure: Draw one maze and distribute, or source from Google Images or elsewhere on the Internet. Ask clients to write affirmations, positive words, and statements in their maze. Next suggest they draw a line demonstrating the way out of the maze. Have them place a small figure or shape somewhere in or out of the maze to represent where they are in terms of their self-esteem. For example, are they about to leave the maze (higher self-esteem), in the middle of it (moderate self-esteem), or just entering the maze or lost in it (low self-esteem)?

Discussion: Discussion focuses on the design of the maze, the words and affirmations that comprise it, and the placement of the figure (the client) in the maze. Goals include exploration of self-esteem and positive thinking.

SELF-ESTEEM EXPLORATION

Materials: Writing paper, pens, pencils, drawing paper, statement sheet for each client, and markers.

Procedure: Have clients read the following statements and rate their response to each statement on a scale of 1–10 (10 is the highest and 1 is the lowest). Next ask them to draw a symbol of their self-esteem using shape and color. For example, someone with positive self-esteem might draw a large, bright shape while someone with poor self-esteem might draw a small, dark form.

- I like myself.
- People seem to like me.
- I have talents.
- I am a good and worthwhile person.
- I will do well in the future.
- I feel well today.
- I feel comfortable at social events.
- I like to be with friends.
- I am good to myself.
- I have hobbies.
- I find time for fun in my life.
- I laugh at least once a day.
- I compliment myself.
- I forgive myself when I make a mistake.
- I eat in a healthy manner.
- I visit the doctor and dentist regularly.
- I exercise.
- I treat myself as I treat others.
- I seek help when I need it.

- I don't have to be validated by others.

- I am allowing myself to learn new things and have new experiences.

- I try to accept change.

- I can accept support from others.

- I can acknowledge my accomplishments.

- I can say no.

- It is okay if I am not perfect.

- I love myself "just because I am me."

Discussion: Discussion focuses on the statement sheet and the significance of the self-esteem drawings. Goals include self-awareness, identification of areas that need to be worked on, and exploration of methods to increase self-esteem.

COMBATING ANXIETY

Materials: Drawing paper, markers, oil pastels, and crayons.

Procedure: Ask clients to examine the following list of ways to combat anxiety and create a collage of photos that represent items on the list. For example, a photo of someone in a yoga pose, someone mediating, a smiling person (being positive), or someone exercising or painting.

Methods of relaxation include:

- deep breathing

- guided imagery

- exercise (walking)

- journaling

- getting enough sleep, eating in a healthy manner (including fruits and vegetables)

- having a positive outlook

- taking "one day at a time"

- taking tiny steps forward

- self-processing (self-talk)

- realizing things are probably temporary (just for now)

- aromatherapy

- acupuncture

- finding support systems

- avoiding caffeine

- practicing yoga

- meditation

- focusing on "the here and now" (being mindful)

- if possible, avoiding people and/or situations that cause stress

- attending therapy

- having a pet

- taking medications as prescribed

- listening to music

- engaging in drawing, painting, needlework, and crafts.

Discussion: Clients explore a variety of ways to reduce stress so that they have a repertoire at their fingertips. Goals include self-soothing and identification of self-help measures.

ACHIEVEMENTS II

Materials: Writing and drawing paper, pens, pencils, markers, and pastels.

Procedure: Ask clients to list their achievements. Then have them create a trophy for their greatest accomplishment. Emphasize that accomplishments can include a wide variety of things such as graduating from school, having a child, serving in the military, being married for many years, keeping their house clean, etc.

Discussion: Discussion focuses on the achievements listed and the design of the trophy. Examine the size, shape, and color/s of the trophy. Ask questions such as: Is the trophy deserved? Is it heavy/light? How does it specifically represent the achievement? Goals include identifying strengths and increasing self-esteem.

VISION BOARD

Materials: Oak tag (poster board) or cardboard (about 12 × 18 inches), magazines, markers, oil pastels crayons, scissors, and glue.

Procedure: Introduce the vision board as a collection of photos, drawings, and words that represent the clients' visions for the future. Group members will select photos, draw pictures and/or use symbols that represent things they'd like to do, places they'd like to go, people they'd like to socialize with, how they'd like to feel, etc. in upcoming years.

Discussion: Discussion focuses on the composition of the vision board and items included in it. Methods to obtain those items, aims, and desires are examined. Goals include identifying objectives, organizing thoughts, and supporting a positive outlook.

SPIRITUALITY

Materials: Drawing paper, question/statement sheets for each participant, oil pastels, markers, and crayons.

Procedure: The procedure is divided into two parts.

Part 1: Ask clients to share their personal definition of spirituality and then have them illustrate their thoughts. Suggest that spirituality can focus on religion, but it can also be a belief in nature, love, art, music, the universe, a higher power, etc.

Part 2: Have clients write brief responses to the following questions/statements and then ask them to share their responses:

1. What customs do you follow? (e.g. holiday customs or daily rituals such as drinking coffee every morning, reading before bed, etc.).

2. What is your inner talk (what do you say to yourself when undecided and in times of stress)?

3. How do you relax?

4. How do you find inner peace?

5. Do you have any special affirmations, mantras, or prayers that help you cope?

6. Describe a few relaxation techniques that you find useful.

7. List here things you are grateful for in your life.

8. What do you find beautiful in nature?

9. How do you stimulate your mind?

10. What is your purpose?

11. Who or what do you love?

12. Do you believe in a higher power? Explain.

Discussion: Clients share their ideas about spirituality and examine how spiritual beliefs can positively affect their lives. Explore how spirituality helps people handle problems, losses, illness, and life's uncertainties. Examine the symbols and the meaning of the artwork presented. Observe similarities and/or differences in the representations. Goals include exploration of the healing power of spirituality, its diversity, and its significance for many individuals.

The following list, compiled by clients, incorporates the benefits of being spiritual:

- "Gives you a purpose."

- "Raises self-esteem."

- "Something to believe in."

- "Better sense of self-worth."

- "Helps get you through the hard times."

- "Gives you more faith and confidence."

- "Can calm you down."

- "Gives you hope."

- "Faith, hope and charity, three theological virtues."

- "Connects you with others, like when you go to church or synagogue."

OPTIMISM

Materials: Writing paper, pens, and pencils.

Procedure: Discuss the saying, "When one door closes another door opens." Ask clients to share a time in their life when "one door closed" but another opened for them (such as getting fired from a job and then finding a better job). Next read the following short story and discuss thoughts and feelings about its meaning:

There is an old Chinese story that tells of a poor farmer who depended on his horse for plowing and getting around. One day the horse left. The neighbors approached him with sadness and talked about how bad it was. The poor farmer said, "Maybe."

The next day the horse returned with two other horses. The neighbors approached him with happiness and talked about how wonderful it was. The poor farmer said, "Maybe."

The next day, the poor farmer's son tried to ride one of the horses and it threw him and broke his leg, rendering him unable to work. The neighbors approached him with sadness to talk about how bad it was. The poor farmer said, "Maybe."

The next day, the army called on the boy to serve. They rejected him because of his broken leg.

Discussion: Discuss the idea of being positive and looking at life with an optimistic attitude. Explore the following questions:

1. Was the farmer an optimist and/or a pragmatist?

2. Did the farmer's attitude help him?

3. How did things turn out for the farmer?

4. What are your thoughts about the neighbor and their reactions to the incidents?

5. How important is it to find "the good" in things?

6. How important is your attitude in determining how good or bad a situation is?

7. Have you ever been in a situation where "the bad" turned into "good?"

8. Have you ever worried about something that didn't end up happening?

9. How do our perspective and attitude affect our happiness?

10. What do you think happened next in the story?

GROWTH

Materials: Pens, pencils, markers, ruler, oil pastels, and crayons.

Procedure: This project may require two sessions depending on the client's focus and lenght of group session. Give the participants the following instructions: "Divide a sheet into four even rows. In the first row draw a tiny object, egg or seedling. In the next three rows show the seedling slowly growing until it is fully developed.

On another sheet of paper use words, sentences, and sketches to show what was needed to nurture this animal, item, figure, or thing.

On the last sheet of paper draw and/or list what you need or will need to nurture yourself so you achieve your potential."

Discussion: Explore necessities and needs, and methods to achieve goals. Explore nurturing techniques.

SELF-ESTEEM PRACTICE

Materials: Pencils and pens.

Procedure: Clients read through the following scenarios and share what could have been done in each circumstance to boost the self-esteem of the individual.

1. Jessica and Bill stayed in a hotel in London for two days. It was almost time to leave so Jessica asked the concierge to call the shuttle bus to take her and Bill to the airport. The shuttle bus was £30.00 less than a taxi. Jessica and Bill had two hours free so they went to breakfast, and packed their bags. When they were ready to leave for the airport they noticed the bus had not arrived. They asked the concierge how much longer it would take for the bus to get to the hotel. The concierge looked sheepish as she apologized and said she was busy and forgot to call the shuttle service. She told the couple that they would have to take the cab. They were furious but they called the taxi company and paid the extra £30.00.

Sample answer: Jessica and Bill could have been assertive and insisted on speaking with the hotel manager. They have could have asked that the extra £30.00 be taken off their hotel bill.

2. Marjorie and Andy visited their friends Lois and Matt. Andy kept criticizing Marjorie, saying she ate too fast, she laughed too loudly, and she was sloppy (after spilling a little juice on her shirt). Marjorie looked hurt but said nothing.

Sample answer: Marjorie could have told Andy in private that she feels hurt when criticized, especially in front of friends. She might have let Andy know that it was important to her that he changes his behavior.

3. Mark decided he didn't like the jeans he bought at a clothes store. He had lost the receipt, but the tags were still on the jeans. He decided not to try to return them since he was missing the receipt.

Sample answer: It would have been helpful if Mark took the healthy risk and attempted to return the jeans. If the sales clerk didn't allow him to return them he could have asked for the sales manager. Most likely he would have received a full refund or at least store credit: "The squeaky wheel gets the oil."

4. Maria has been dating Chris for five years. She would like to get married and she desperately wants to have children. Chris tells Mary he might not be ready to settle down for at least five more years and he is not sure whether or not he wants to have children. He says he might need to have an open relationship for a while. Mary is very aware that her biological clock is ticking. She tells Chris she will wait as long as it takes for him to make a commitment.

Sample answer: Mary could ask to have a heart to heart talk with Chris and tell him her strong feelings about matrimony and family. If he stays firm she could tell him she will give him an allotted time to think about it but then move on with her life. She needs to explore her own priorities.

5. Samantha is queuing in the supermarket and another woman cuts right in front of her saying, "Sorry I am in a rush." Samantha obliges although she has to get back to work.

Sample answer: Samantha could have told the woman, "No, I am in a hurry too."

6. Michael always compares himself with others and he usually feels inadequate. Last week he felt very badly because his friend Bradley bought a new car and he has an old car that is often problematic.

Sample answer: Michael needs to start focusing on himself and not on others. He is just setting himself up for disappointment and anxiety. When you compare yourself to others it is a "lose-lose" situation. There will always be someone smarter, richer, etc. Michael might have thought, "In the future I'll have a new car too; I'm okay with what I presently have." He might have said "So what?" to himself.

7. Dan was a salesman for many years and won various awards over the years. One day he made an error and was reprimanded by his boss. Dan decided he was worthless and a very poor worker.

Sample answer: Dan could have thought, "Next time I will do better, after all my track record is excellent. Everyone makes mistakes sometimes; I am only human."

8. Gloria received a grade C on a history exam. She was appalled since she usually receives As and expected an A on this test. Gloria was devastated. She was so upset she didn't go to her best friend's party and stayed in the house all weekend feeling sorry for herself.

Sample answer: Gloria might have been disappointed but she could have handled her disappointment in a more constructive way. She could have processed the situation and maintained control by coming up with a plan of action. Perhaps next time she might begin studying a few more days or weeks before the test or next time she might get more sleep or eat breakfast the morning of the test. After exploring what she did wrong she could practice better study habits so that she does better next time. She is wasting all of her good energy with self-pity. She would have been much better off relaxing and going to the party; she could choose to allow herself to be fallible once in a while.

Discussion: Participants discuss positive behaviors and ways they relate to behavior and attitude depicted in the descriptions.

POSITIVE PICTURE PASS

Materials: Magazine photos, drawing paper, pens, pencils, scissors, and glue sticks.

Procedure: This project may require two sessions to complete. Participants find as many uplifting photos as there are clients in the group (so if there are eight clients in a group, each participant finds eight photos). Next each person signs their first name at the bottom of a piece of drawing paper and places the first photo on that sheet of paper. Emphasize to participants that the photos should not be too large because each sheet has to include photos from all group members. In this case, eight photos would need to fit on each sheet of paper. The group leader waits a few seconds and then says, "Pass," and each person gives the paper he just worked on to the person to his right and glues the next photo on the sheet passed to him. The papers go round the room in the same manner until each person receives his original paper back. He knows it is the original because his name is on the bottom of the page. When he receives his paper back it will be filled with positive pictures.

Discussion: Each individual will be asked to comment on the completed collage and point out the parts of it that are eye catching and/or significant. Other group members will comment and try to relate to the positive pictures.

This is a very non-threatening and enjoyable exercise. Self-esteem is immediately increased as individuals connect with one another and share thoughts and feelings.

KINDNESS

Materials: Template of a profile of a face, markers, pens, and pencils.

Procedure: Participants trace the template of the profile. Next they are asked to fill it in with a variety of ways to demonstrate self-respect, kindness, and self-care. Examples include:

1. buying oneself flowers

2. cooking for oneself

3. exercising

4. allowing mistakes to happen

5. not berating oneself

6. getting enough sleep

7. choosing one's battles

8. not dwelling on what is out of one's control

9. eating nutritiously

10. positive self-talk.

Discussion: Explore the importance of self-loving and self-soothing attitudes and practices. Discuss methods to increase self-approval, and decrease stress and self-deprecation.

IMPROVING RELATIONSHIPS II

Materials: Writing paper, pens, and pencils.

Procedure: Relationships affect all aspects of our lives and life satisfaction. They affect family and friends, co-workers, and people we come across in supermarkets and so on in everyday life. Relationships can leave us isolated and depressed or lift our spirits and provide warmth and love, especially in times of crisis. It is up to us to learn how to communicate effectively with others and nurture our relationships. They play a large role in our self-esteem.

Ask participants to list tips for improving relationships. What is needed to enhance them and keep them strong? Ask participants which qualities they look for in a friend and what positive characteristics they bring to a relationship. Have them describe an "ideal" friendship or relationship. After clients have come up with their own list have them take turns reading from the following ideas and commenting about the effectiveness of the tips. Ask if they have been following some of the advice presented. Encourage them to describe their relationships goals.

1. Be a good listener.

2. Empathize.

3. Avoid attacking the other person.

4. Don't make threats or aggressive gestures.

5. Comment on the positive—show support.

6. Respect boundaries.

7. Demonstrate respect towards the other person.

8. Compromise.

9. Choose your battles.

10. Share interests.

11. Be flexible.

12. Keep expectations realistic.

13. Give your friend/partner the benefit of the doubt.

14. Be flexible—it can't always be your way.

15. Show kindness and be thoughtful.

16. Take a step back when angry. Take a deep breath and remove yourself from the situation until you cool off and can think more clearly.

17. Apologize; take the risk of admitting when you are wrong. Would you rather be happy or right?

Discussion: Explore the importance of relationships and methods to maintain and improve them.

INCREASING SELF-ESTEEM: TAKING ACTION[9]

Materials: Writing paper, pens, and pencils

Procedure: This project has two parts and may require two sessions to complete. Instruct group members to answer the following:

Part 1: Preparation

1. What do you appreciate about yourself?

2. What can you do this week that benefits you in some way or that you enjoy doing? (in addition to attending therapy groups).

3. How can you help others? (By helping others you help yourself.)

4. Begin a gratitude list.

Part 2: Action

• Make a list of the things you enjoy doing.

• Make a list of the people you know and have known who bring you pleasure.

• Make a list of your achievements (no matter how small).

- Make a list of positive affirmations. (You may use the list below to help you decide.)

Affirmations:

1. I will do my best and leave myself alone.

2. I am fine just the way I am.

3. I love myself.

4. I will take one day at a time.

5. No one can make me feel badly about myself except me.

6. I will be mindful.

7. I will forgive myself.

8. I am grateful for each day.

9. My mind is calm.

10. I am strong.

11. I am determined.

12. Everything is getting better every day.

13. I am worthy.

14. I embrace positive self-esteem.

15. I have inner resources.

16. I will be happy with who I am and what I have.

17. I will focus on what is in my control.

18. I will take care of my body by exercising and eating well.

19. I will nourish my mind and soul.

20. I choose to be happy.

21. I choose who is in my life and how I react to what they say and do.

22. I see each part of life as a lesson.

23. My thoughts are under my control.

24. I will be in the moment. I will think about the positive things in my life.

25. I am appreciated.

26. I have choices in life; opportunities surround me.

27. I will take healthy risks.

28. I am allowed to make mistakes.

29. I change what I can and I don't dwell on what I can't.

30. Feel it, process it and let it go.[5]

Discussion: Participants share positive characteristics and experiences. Encourage them to find a few affirmations they can apply to their everyday life and review each day to raise hope and self-worth.

SINGING KARAOKE[12]

Materials: Karaoke machine, microphone, karaoke CDs, and a booklet of available songs that group members can select a song from.

Procedure: "Set up some karaoke rules: Respect each other. Don't laugh at the singer or make fun of the song that was selected. No talking during the song. Practice the DBT skill of being non-judgmental.

Each person will get a chance to select a song. When it's someone's turn that person can decide whether they want to sing alone on the microphone or sing all together as a group."

Discussion: "One of the DBT skills that raises self-esteem is called Building Mastery. Its one of the emotion regulation skills, and the concept is to do something a little bit challenging to make yourself feel more competent. Sometimes a client feels shy about singing at first so they start out just listening. Then soon they are singing along with the group. Often, in time, they choose to sing alone on the microphone. I've heard many clients say 'I wanted to make myself do this even though I was nervous, just to prove to myself that I can do it.' (The DBT skill of Opposite Action) They felt proud.

Karaoke is an easy, fairly inexpensive way for a group to have a sing along where all are involved. It's nice that the lyrics can be viewed on the TV screen for all to see. "[6]

IDENTITY MAP[7]

Materials: Drawing paper, markers, pencils, and pens.

Procedure: Suggest that clients create a map completely about them. They may add anything they desire including: whatever they love/enjoy, buildings, streets, parks, signs, family members, friends, hobbies and interests, places of interest in their neighborhood, goals, memories, hopes, etc. The map may be named after they are finished.

Discussion: Self-awareness is a key component of self-esteem. It is important to understand one's goals, beliefs, desires, likes, and dislikes. It is essential to understand how people, places, and things contribute to mood, motivation, and feelings of self-worth. Creating an identity maps helps individuals recognize major areas of their life that provide satisfaction and/or that need improvement.

AMULET[8]

Materials: Drawing paper, construction paper, magazine photos, markers, oil pastels, scissors, glue, felt, pipe cleaners, and other collage materials.

Procedure: Clients create an amulet for themselves or another individual. They may design the amulet in any way they please using a variety of collage materials if desired.

am·u·let (15), **noun** \àm-yə-lət\ A small object worn to ward off evil, harm, or illness or to bring good fortune; protecting charm.[9]

Discussion: Participants share methods to protect themselves from physical and/or psychological harm. The amulet can be explored as a metaphor for self-preservation and strength. Creating amulets may give clients a sense of control and hope. Examine how various coping skills can be considered psychological amulets.

NOTES

1. Modified from an idea by the Kennedy Center Arts Edge, "A Character Life Box." See http://artsedge.kennedy-center.org/educators/lessons/grade-6-8/Character_Life_Box.aspx, accessed on 9 October 2014.
2. Modified from an idea by Tracylynn Navarro, ATR-BC, Princeton House, University Medical Center at Princeton.
3. Michael Bell, celebrity artist, www.mbellart.com, accessed on 9 October 2014.
4. Boxes may be purchased from S&S Worldwide, www.ssww.com, accessed on 9 October 2014.
5. "Feel it, process it, and let it go" coined by the author, circa 1980.
6. This activity was contributed by Deborah Spiegel MT-BC, DBT informed Board Certified Music Therapist, taken from her book: *Music Activities & More for Teaching DBT Skills and Enhancing Any Therapy: Even for the Non-Musician* (2010) Authorhouse, www.dbtmusic.com, accessed on 9 October 2014.
7. Modified directive from http://fromyourdesks.com/2010/12/06/aaron-meshon/, accessed on 9 October 2014.
8. The amulet theme was inspired from the work of Laura Mecklenburger, MFA, who creates art inspired by the natural world, often to serve as protective armor or a transformative tool for herself and others. According to Mecklenburger, among other works, "I made ceramic and mixed media amulets and ritual vessels designed for specific people I knew." www.cleavermagazine.com/vulnerary-and-an-art-witch-by-laura-mecklenburger/, accessed on 9 October 2014.
9. http://dictionary.reference.com/browse/amulet?s=t, accessed on 9 October 2014.

CHAPTER 9

How to Lead a Healthier, Happier, More Fulfilling Life

This chapter is a condensed version of therapeutic interventions, positive thinking, affirmations, and helpful suggestions. It is written in a different format to the rest of the book because it is intended to be a reader-friendly guide. My goal is to introduce self-help measures and practical, everyday advice in order to enhance the reader's self-awareness, self-esteem, problem-solving skills and day-to-day living. Having a strong ego, sense of self-worth, and optimism, for the future makes a great impact on one's mood, attitude, motivation, goals, relationships, and life style choices. For instance, it is important to learn that taking healthy risks—such as applying for a new job or going on an airplane even though you may be fearful of flying—is an important part of life and that the *process* of living is what important, not so much the end product (wealth, expensive home, achieving a specific goal, etc.). The end product is the icing on the cake, but character is built through the work involved in trying to achieve the objective. The objective might vanish one day (e.g. you could lose a house, get fired from a desired job) but you always have the strength and perseverance you needed to achieve it.

We are always in process and that is how we learn and grow. This type of thinking makes failure more palatable and less bruising to the ego. When we understand that life is an ongoing series of experiences and making mistakes is not the real problem—the real problem is when we *give up* after a mistake is made—we gain insight and command. The strong person gets back up when he falls, and tries multiple times when he fails. The powerful person attempts to transform negative circumstances into more positive ones. In this way he takes command of the situation and doesn't become a victim.

People have more power than they think. We have the power to make many life choices and to decide how we will react to our choices and to the cards we are dealt. We decide how to respond to others, our environment, and our circumstances.

TAKE ONE DAY AT A TIME

Focus on what is going on today. Try to get through this day without concerning yourself with what tomorrow has in store for you. This will help you focus and ease anxiety. Thinking about tomorrow and the next day, and the next can increase stress and become overwhelming. It can become incapacitating and may stop you from doing what needs to be done. This does not mean you can't have future goals and plans; it means you will not dwell or worry about them, especially when you are feeling tired, depressed, or vulnerable.

Eva's house was a mess. There was clutter, bills, and dirty clothes in all the rooms. The thought of cleaning the house seemed overwhelming to Eva. These unpleasant feelings continued and Eva's house became messier and messier. The worse the house looked the less willing she was to clean it. She was at a loss for what to do. Eva began feeling increasingly anxious and depressed. Her self-esteem suffered because she felt guilty about her inability to mobilize herself. At last her friend Barbara came to assist her. Barbara's suggestion was to clean a little bit every day and "Take one day at a time." With Barbara's support Eva began with her bedroom. She allotted one hour a day to clean it, and would leave what she didn't finish for the next day. She began by picking up all the clothes on the floor, then she organized her make-up and beauty supplies. Lastly she vacuumed and dusted. By following this pattern Eva was eventually able to clean her bedroom and every other room in her house. She learned that if she worked slowly, doing a little at a time, it was not so overwhelming and would eventually get done.

Max had many health issues. He had to have blood work biweekly and he frequently visited an array of doctors. There were weeks when Max had three or four doctor appointments, sometimes two in one day. Max often felt depressed and defeated. The visits seemed endless. He was tired of being poked and prodded, and spending so much of his life in waiting rooms. On Mondays he experienced a feeling of dread as he thought about what he had to endure the rest of the week. Max's focus on his unpleasant upcoming schedule of appointments made it difficult for him to cope; he didn't want to get out of bed in the morning and face the day. Life was a chore and extremely depressing. Max needed to think differently and change his coping mechanisms. When he learned to focus on what he had to do each day, and not on his weekly or monthly schedule, he felt better. Life was more doable. His self-talk was that he'd get through "today" and worry about "tomorrow, tomorrow."

LIVE IN THE MOMENT

Focus on what is happening now. Be mindful. The past is gone and we don't know what the future will bring; all we have is the now, the present. Think about what you are doing and who you are with. Try not to let your thoughts wander too much. Get as much enjoyment as you can from your experiences. Treasure the special moments.

BE MINDFUL

Being mindful entails being in the moment and fully utilizing all of your senses. Try to be aware of what you are doing and who you are with. Think about what you are seeing, touching, smelling, and feeling. Be conscious of what your body is feeling and the messages it is conveying to you. Really taste that food, feel the texture of sand, soil, clay, soft hair, etc. Breathe in the fresh air, inhale scintillating scents of perfumes and flowers, and fragrant aromas of delectable dishes. When you take a shower take the time to actually feel how wonderful the water feels on your skin and how soothing the warmth is to your body and spirit. When you chew, savor the taste and flavor of your food. Focus on your partner's essence, his eyes skin, smell, and touch. Don't work too hard controlling your thoughts; allow them to gently float away.

TREASURE TIME WITH FRIENDS AND FAMILY

Appreciate the love you have in your life and those most dear to you. Make time to visit with friends and family, and work hard to keep in touch. Even a quick text message, email, or phone call can be enough to let others know you are thinking of them. Let those close to you know what they mean to you: support, compliment, boost their morale. Treat family members as if they are gold because that is exactly what they are: precious jewels.

FORGIVE EASILY

Harboring a grudge and staying angry creates stress, anxiety, and dissatisfaction with life. It takes away from the enjoyment you are entitled to. It can increase blood pressure and generate symptoms such as headaches, dizziness, chest pains, and stomach aches. It may alienate you from those you care for most. You do not have to forget, but when you forgive someone you are gaining control of your life. The anger is not defining who you are or how you act any more; you become more relaxed and focused on more pleasant thoughts. Your life immediately improves and you feel freer to concentrate on moving forward.

DON'T HOLD GRUDGES

Holding a grudge is like having a weight attached to your chest. It increases stress and anxiety, and actually weighs you down. Pay careful attention to your physical feelings and emotions. Ask yourself:

- Are you benefiting in any way from holding the grudge?
- Is it hurting you?
- Are you experiencing headaches or other stress-related symptoms?
- Are you happy or sad, depressed or frustrated?
- Are you missing out because of this grudge?
- Is the grudge getting you what you want?
- Is there another way to get your needs met?
- What happens if you choose to give up the grudge?

LET GO OF ANGER

Everyone gets angry. If someone says they don't get angry they are either in denial or lying. Some people may not realize they are angry. They try to hide it, but it always comes out. It may come out in a depression, anxiety attacks, headaches, or gastrointestinal problems. Since anger is normal we will all experience it, but the key is *what to do about it*. Anger is toxic if held onto for too long. It eats away at you physically and emotionally. Expressing your anger in a calm manner is the most effective way to release it and to get others to listen to you.

If you are aggressive (yelling, cursing, hitting, punching the wall, etc.) others will discount you and become immediately defensive. They may ignore you, run away, cry, call for help, or appease you but not really mean it. You will not be taken seriously and you will lose respect. If you become too angry too quickly, walk out of the room.

Remove yourself from the situation for a while until you have time to calm down and think about what you want to say. Take a walk, exercise, jog around the block, listen to music, or go to the gym. You may even want to write your thoughts on a piece of paper so that you will remember everything you want to say in a clear and focused manner.

If you are passive (ignoring problems, not confronting issues) others will take advantage of you and your needs will not be met. Your self-esteem may suffer because your voice is not heard. You lose out in life.

If you are assertive (saying what you feel in a strong but calm manner) most people will listen and take what you say very seriously. You have a much better chance of being heard and getting your needs met. Don't be afraid of letting someone know if you need something, if they hurt your feelings, or did something wrong.

Make sure to ask questions and don't allow doctors or anyone else to intimidate you. Doctors are just people with advanced degrees and specialized training. Try your best to pursue things you feel strongly about. Just remember you can catch more flies with honey than with vinegar.

BE OPTIMISTIC

When you look at the bright side of life you feel better physically and emotionally. Sometimes self-fulfilling prophesies come true. If you focus on a situation working out in a positive manner there is a better chance of it actually working out than if you have a negative outlook. For instance, if you are applying for a job and you say to yourself you will get the job, you will go into that office with a brighter smile and more self-confidence. That might clinch the job. If you walk into the interview thinking you are not good enough and that you probably won't get the job, the employer may notice negativity or view you as someone with low self-worth and not give you the job.

Focus on what you have as opposed to what you want or need. Focus on your strengths, not your weaknesses. Concentrate more on the possibilities and fun you can have instead of your problems and worries. Use your energy to work on ways to improve your situation instead of using it to aggravate and berate yourself.

THINK POSITIVELY[1]

When you think in a positive manner you become happier. One major position in the cognitive behavioral triangle is that feelings are elicited by your thoughts. You decide how you are going to react to situations and what your mood will be like. You can choose to see a situation from the negative point of view or the positive. What's important to know is that it is up to you—*you decide*. Even if you are challenged with an illness, you can decide how to handle your feelings, behavior, and actions. You can choose to curl up on the couch and retreat from society or deal with the illness and do the best you can. *You can focus on what is in your control as opposed to what's out of your control.*

If you are feeling blue you can go with the feeling and isolate, or work towards overcoming the feeling. When you smile, for instance, people are more attracted to you and you feel better. Smiling or laughing changes the chemistry in your body and you actually feel better, even if the smile or laughter is forced. Life usually seems brighter when you think things will turn out for the best. Hope is crucial for survival.

TAKE THE FIRST STEP

Be the first one to make the phone call or apologize. Be the first one to introduce yourself to a newcomer at work or at a party. Stand up for what you believe in. Share novel thoughts and feelings. Don't be a follower. Do what you think is right and be brave. Sometimes it takes a very courageous person to make the first move towards reconciliation.

EMPATHIZE

Try to see the other person's point of view. For a few seconds pretend you are experiencing what he is experiencing. How would you feel and react? This will help you understand others' feelings, actions, and behaviors. It may help you better handle tricky situations and rocky relationships. It will make you more understanding and supportive, and a better son/daughter, mother/father, sister/brother, partner, co-worker, and friend.

TAKE HEALTHY RISKS

If you play it safe your whole life you won't grow, you won't have much excitement, and you may not experience all that life has to offer. Sometimes you will win and sometimes you will lose, but at least you will know that you have tried; that is what is important. For instance, if you write a book and you are afraid it won't get published, and therefore you never attempt to find a publisher, you'll never know what could have been. Maybe you could have been a famous author. If you are afraid to speak to women/men at parties because of fear of rejection, and therefore never have meaningful relationships, you might miss out on something wonderful.

Life is full of risks. Unhealthy risks might include bungee jumping, parachuting from a plane, race car driving, and the like. These are risky because the chance of injury and/or death is greatly increased. Healthy risks often boost your self-esteem and are generally safe. These include asking someone for a date, applying for a new job, speaking in front of an audience, sharing novel thoughts, making a move, etc. Thinking outside of the box is a healthy risk.

FORGIVE YOURSELF

It is crucial to let go of guilt and forgive yourself. Guilt is extremely unhealthy. It increases anxiety and lowers self-esteem. Learn from the guilt and your mistakes, but then allow the guilt to dissipate; let it go.

Feel it, process it and let it go.

To feel guilty is to stay in the past. It keeps you stuck and helpless. Instead of wallowing in your guilt, work towards remedying the situation and/or making yourself into a better person. Set up a plan of action; make amends. You and those around you will be happier and healthier. We cannot change the past but we can make the present and the future a brighter place.

BE KIND TO YOURSELF

You are your own best friend; you are very important. Be kind to yourself. Treat yourself as well as you treat others (or better). Don't berate yourself; forgive yourself; support and compliment yourself for a job well done. Support yourself for trying and for taking healthy risks. Leave yourself alone when you fail or make mistakes; you are only human. Forgive yourself for weaknesses; no one is perfect. Focus on your strengths and achievements, no matter how small. Don't wait for others to do for you, *do for yourself.* If no one acknowledges your birthday, buy your own cake; take yourself to the movies or out to dinner. Buy yourself a bouquet of flowers; take yourself on a vacation or day trip. Make a fancy meal for yourself and freeze the leftovers for another day; make your bedroom as comfortable and lovely as possible; you are worth it. Make the best of bad situations by looking on the bright side. Make yourself as relaxed and cheerful as you can; it's your responsibility to take care of your physical and mental health, and overall well-being.

KEEP LEARNING

It is important to learn and grow throughout your life. It will keep you young, strong, healthy, fresh, and full of zest. Your memory will be better and your thinking will be stronger. Your self-esteem will be higher and you will be more interesting. Keep up to date on the news and on technological and scientific breakthroughs. Read; watch the news; listen to various points of view before formulating your opinion. Keep an open mind. Learn about various periods in history or learn a new language. Visit museums, see movies and plays, go to art shows, visit other cities, states, or countries, write, create, collect, design, build, plant, audit college classes, mentor, volunteer, live life to its fullest.

DO THE JOB YOU ENJOY

If you work full time you are working most of your life. The average person works eight hours a day, five days a week. That is 40 hours of work per week, 160 hours a month and 1,920 hours a year. If you are not enjoying your work, you are wasting much of your life doing something that is tedious or annoying. That is awfully sad. Sometimes we have little control about what do. This may be due to financial or marital situations, the economy, or our academic achievements. Yet a lot of people choose their jobs or professions for the wrong reasons. Some people do what they think is expected of them, such as a person becoming a doctor because his parents want him to practice medicine. Some people take a job for the money such as someone who becomes a certified public accountant (CPA) when he would rather paint, and some people take the easy way out, perhaps taking a simple nine to five job with little responsibility instead of pursuing their dream job, which would entail taking a risk. This way failure is not an option.

If possible, try to do what you like or love: what you are passionate about. Then you will feel valuable and purposeful. Going to work each day will be more of a pleasure than a chore. It won't seem like you are wasting your life away.

LIVE FOR YOURSELF: IT'S YOUR LIFE

You only get one life, so live it to its fullest. It's your life, not your mother's or your father's life, or your husband's life. You need to live it in the way you see fit. Try not to feel pressured to lead a certain life style or maintain certain opinions because others are pressuring you to live or think in a specific way. They are living their life, now you live yours. For instance:

- Your friends may all go out on Saturday nights and perhaps you like to stay home and watch television. Try not to feel pressured to go out because that's what they do. Think about what you really like to do and do it. Stay home, relax, and watch television; it's okay.

- If you are dating someone of a different faith and friends or relatives dislike this, remember that it is your life and your decision. They can share what is on their mind, but they cannot dictate how you live unless you allow them to do so. If he is a good person, date him.

- You do not have to be like your neighbors or live like them. If all of your neighbors buy a fence it doesn't mean you need to buy one too. Maybe you prefer trees or bushes to fences. That's okay.

- If all of your friends are having large weddings, it's fine for you to have a small gathering. Do what is right and comfortable for you.

- If it is a sunny day and you notice a lot of joggers and cyclists outside, and you'd rather stay in and read, don't feel pressured to go outside.

Do what you feel like doing, it's okay. You do not have to please others or do what others do. Be your authentic self in order to feel satisfied and most contented.

ASK FOR HELP WHEN YOU NEED IT

It is not always easy asking for support. Sometimes during our life we are the helpers and at other times we are the ones in need of help, the *helpee*. Occasionally the roles can vary, and other times it may take years before an individual becomes the helpee. It takes strength and courage to hold both positions. Sometimes it takes more strength to request help than to provide it. The intelligent individual will ask for help because he will usually get his needs met quicker and will most likely end off healthier. There is no need to suffer in silence; swallow your pride and work towards wellness. Survival of the fittest includes being smart and knowing when to turn to others for assistance. In one therapy group a young man stated that "You are never the helpee because when you are receiving help you are helping yourself."

TRY TO BE FLEXIBLE

Stay away from *all or nothing* thinking and life will be more pleasant. Nothing in this world is black or white; it is important to be able to see the gray area. Do you always have to have things your way? Can you give in at least a little to create harmony? Discuss how you and your partner can work together to come to some sort of agreement. Perhaps you can give in occasionally. Does everything in your life have to be perfect? Are you intolerant of others' shortcomings? Staying rigid keeps you from experiencing new things, finding new interests, and developing friendships. It stops you from relaxing and just enjoying the moment. You may think you are in control, but you lose power when you are unyielding. You are at the mercy of everyone and everything around you. No one will meet all of your expectations; everyone has their foibles. Focus on the positives instead of the negatives. Choose your battles; *is it better to be right or to have a good friendship, partnership, or marriage?*

BE ASSERTIVE

Calmly express your thoughts and needs. Be strong but not loud. Be consistent and persistent, but not obsessive. When you let others know what your needs are they are more likely to be met, and it is less likely that anyone will take advantage of you; you will feel better about yourself. For example, the assertive individual will try to get the job even though he may be a drop under qualified; the assertive person will confront someone who is rude to him; he'll tell his doctor he doesn't understand what is being said to him and ask for clarification. He'll enter a contest, run a race, travel, and try to do a variety of things he never experienced before. People will not take advantage of the assertive individual; he will not allow others to treat him in an unfair, negative, or demeaning manner.

PRAISE YOURSELF

Give yourself credit for your accomplishments, no matter how small. Praise yourself for talking care of your health and well-being. Congratulate yourself for being responsible and going to work or school each day. Commend yourself for being a good partner, friend, husband, wife, brother, sister, worker, etc. Applaud yourself when you take healthy risks, and when you do annoying errands or chores. Commend yourself for a job well done. Admire yourself for being you and accept yourself as you are. Applaud your uniqueness and special qualities.

EXERCISE

Do some sort of exercise on at least three days a week. Walk, run, lift weights, dance, play tennis, etc. Keep as active as possible, even if it means standing up while speaking on the phone or parking far away from your destination. Walk up the stairs, don't take the elevator, and get up to change the channel on the television instead of using the remote. Don't work on the computer too long without *movement breaks*. Exercise helps keep you young and strong. It helps strengthen your bones, lowers blood pressure and cholesterol, increases a sense of well-being, and increases energy and strength. For some people walking or running, for instance, may work as well as antidepressants when mild depression sets in. It may help improve your memory and ward off diseases like cancer, Alzheimer's disease, and heart disease.

EAT NUTRITIOUS FOODS

You may enjoy a few goodies such as pizza or cake over the weekend, but for the most part *eat to live*, don't *live to eat*. Try a Mediterranean type of diet where your focus is on fish, vegetables, fruits, nuts, and whole grains (brown products, not white). Chicken is okay a few times a week, and lean meat might be an acceptable choice once a week or bi-weekly. Mainly drink water and stay away from sugary juices and soda. Don't let yourself go hungry but snack wisely. Healthy snacks such as almond butter, natural peanut butter and wheat crackers, beans, carrots, ices (low sugar), low fat yogurt, and a small handful of nuts, oatmeal packets, low salt/fat soup, and fruit would be wise choices. When you eat in a healthy manner you generally feel more energized and your self-esteem increases because you are taking good care of yourself.

DON'T SETTLE

You are special so don't settle unless there is no other choice or you realize you are being much too picky. Be realistic but don't give up easily. Try to get the most out of life. Don't underestimate you strengths and potential; "Go for it." Try to date that exceptional someone; try to get that spectacular job; go on that wonderful vacation if you can afford it; buy the larger, more desirable house if you can afford it and it makes you happy. Get an advanced degree; keep on learning even when you are older; keep trying to perfect whatever it is you are working on at the time. Persevere because you never know what you can accomplish and what life has in store for you. If you don't try you won't ever know if you could have succeeded.

VISIT THE DOCTOR AS NEEDED

Sometimes we would like to be like the ostrich and stick our head in the sand, but we have to take responsibility for our health. Go to the doctor every two years or so for a regular check-up.

Know your cholesterol and blood pressure numbers. When you are age appropriate have specific tests done such as a colonoscopy and mammogram. Visit the dentist bi-yearly. If you don't feel well, don't wait too long; it can't hurt to let a professional take a peek. It will ease your mind, and remember, *better safe than sorry.*

DON'T BE AFRAID TO ASK; THE SQUEAKING WHEEL GETS THE OIL

If you don't speak up, no one knows you have a need or problem. Let others know what you desire or are displeased about. You will probably have greater self-esteem and contentment if you share your thoughts and feelings. For example, if you want a promotion ask for it or suggest ways the company can thrive; if you want a neighbor to drive you to the store, ask him. The worst that can happen is that he says no. If you are having symptoms, let the doctor know. If you are unhappy with how your partner is behaving, tell him. Being assertive will help you lead a more meaningful and richer life.

APPRECIATE WHAT YOU HAVE

Instead of thinking about the things you don't have, think about the things you do have. Appreciate all the gifts and treasures in your life. Think about what is really important in this world. Be grateful for your family, friends, health, your job and/or volunteer position. Appreciate the fact that you can help others and you can call on others to help you. Be thankful for the sunrise and sunset, for the stars, sun, and Mother Nature. Appreciate a restful night's sleep or delightful nap. Be grateful for food, water, ice cream, and hot coffee, tea, or hot chocolate on a cold winter's day. Be mindful of all you possess and the unique people in your life.

DON'T ENVY OTHERS

Everything looks brighter on the other side of the fence. However, when you look more carefully there may be a lot of holes and weeds there. The backyard may be in a shambles. When you begin to envy others remember you never know what is really going on in their life or what they have experienced in the past: *looks can be deceiving*. A person may appear "perfect" but underneath his good looks may be an anxiety-ridden or depressed individual. A family may appear ideal, but the husband or wife may be frustrated, anxious, or having an affair. He or she may be an addict or cruel and abusive. The bottom line is *you never know*. If you want what others have, watch out, you may just get it. Envy will leave you frustrated, angry, and jealous. You will never be satisfied and you won't take time to appreciate all you do have in your life. It is much healthier to focus your energies on yourself and what *you* possess and experience. Try to be the best you can be, enjoy each day, and don't dwell on the accomplishments of your friends, co-workers or neighbors. Take pleasure in your own rewards, friends, and family. Celebrate your uniqueness and strengths.

ACCEPT YOURSELF UNCONDITIONALLY

Love yourself regardless of your achievements, appearance, wealth, or health. Love yourself because you are you: a unique and special individual. Accept that you are a human being with positive and negative characteristics. You will make mistakes just like everyone else does; no one is perfect. Try to forgive yourself and move on. Be kind to yourself; don't dwell on any weaknesses or faults. Don't berate yourself for poor choices or errors. *Process them, learn from them, and then let them go.* Treasure your strengths and all that you have to give and share with others. Instead of being critical, build yourself up, and focus on what you can attain instead of what you didn't or can't attain. Look at yourself in the mirror each day and recite a few affirmations such as:

- I am good enough.

- I am unique and special.

- I have a lot to offer.

- I am a worthwhile person.

- I am the master of my fate.

- I am worthy.

- I am proud of myself for trying.

- I love and accept myself.

- It's okay to make mistakes; I learn from my mistakes.

- I am brave.

- I take healthy risks.

- I will not give up.

- I will not compare myself to others.

- I will take one day at a time.

- I am in charge of my self-talk; I can think positively about myself if I choose to do so.

- I am unique and have my own style.

- Change what you can but don't dwell on what you can't change.

- Life is a process, this too shall pass.

LAUGH AS MUCH AS POSSIBLE

Laughter is the best medicine. Laughing provides a sense of relief and energy. It is stimulating and just plain old fun. Laughing can actually change the body chemistry so depression lifts (at least for a short while). It helps maintain and invigorate relationships and your overall health. It can be a workout for your heart. When you laugh you may gain a better perspective; you don't take yourself or others so seriously. An argument may seem less stressful and less upsetting after a good laugh. Laughter helps diffuse disagreements and quarrels. Laughing gets your mind off your troubles; it is like a mini vacation. When you laugh you are in the moment; you are not thinking of your worries and concerns. It's okay to be silly sometimes (given the proper place and time). Don't lose the child within you; that child will keep you young, playful, and joyful.

If you don't feel like you can laugh watch a funny movie or television show, or try to be with people who make you smile. Read a humorous book or practice something that is fun but difficult to do, like juggling. That should put a smile on your face and on the faces of those around you. Learn a joke and tell it to friends and family to do the same. Do an everyday activity but use your less dominant hand. You may laugh at your clumsiness or how strange it may feel to do an everyday task in a different manner. Continue to attempt to find the humor in life in as many ways as possible.

COMPLIMENT WHEN IT IS DESERVED

Saying something supportive to someone is free of charge and it makes the other person feel positive. It also makes you feel better about yourself. Don't be stingy with those kind words and gestures. You have more control than you realize. You can increase the self-esteem of others and help them have a more pleasant day. The individual who receives the compliment may, in turn, be more supportive of people he meets. The Butterfly Effect may take place and before you know it you have helped dozens of people because of one small act of kindness.

INCREASE THE SELF-ESTEEM OF THOSE YOU LOVE

Be especially kind and considerate to those closest to you. Even if you disagree with their opinions, respect what they have to say. Listen carefully to what is being shared with you. Don't discount their point of view or their feelings. Support them when they are in trouble, conflicted, or feeling down. Compliment them about their achievements perseverance, personality, sense of humor, appearance, jobs, and favors they do for you, no matter how small. Thank them for doing errands and chores around the house. Let them know you think highly of them and admire them. At least once a day let those you love know how much they mean to you. Everyone likes to be appreciated.

TALK IT OUT, DON'T HOLD IT IN

When you feel angry or annoyed with a family member express your feelings. Let the other person know how you feel and have a discussion to resolve the issue. When you hold in your feelings nothing gets resolved and you begin to harbor resentment against the other person. The other person feels your anger and starts to become annoyed with you. The situation escalates. When you hold in your feelings they frequently emerge as symptoms such as headaches, stomach aches, anxiety, dizziness, and trouble sleeping. You may feel tired, irritable, and somewhat depressed. It is not healthy physically or psychologically to keep problems to yourself. Relationships suffer and your quality of life diminishes.

FOCUS ON THE PRESENT

It is always a good idea to have a savings account and to plan for what may lay ahead in future years. The trick is not to dwell on what may happen five, ten, or twenty years from now. Thinking too much about the future may increase anxiety and stress. It can seem overwhelming to think of what life will be like when you are older. The healthiest way to live a satisfying life is to focus on the present. The present time is all we have; we don't know what will happen in years to come. Be mindful and enjoy each day as much as possible. If you are financially able, take that vacation now, buy that home, treat yourself to the new computer or latest television set; don't put it off. Wear your jewelry or fine clothes and take pleasure in them;

go to that show, attend that concert, even if it is a bit pricey; get on that plane and visit with family and friends. Enjoy yourself as much as possible as long as it is healthy and you are not hurting anyone. Be the finest person you can and do your best *now*, but continue to add to your repertoire of positive achievements and experiences as time goes by.

DON'T THINK ABOUT THE FRIGHTENING POSSIBILITIES IN LIFE

Life can be precarious and scary at times. If you start dwelling on all the things that could happen to you or to the country/world such has another war, terrorist attacks, super volcanoes, etc. you may become extremely stressed, or at the least you will most likely experience an array of anxiety symptoms. When your mind begins to wander and your thoughts are becoming too negative, work towards thought stopping. Say "Stop" to yourself and immediately change your mindset. Begin thinking about something that makes you feel serene and positive such as lying on a sunny beach or being with those you love. After some practice this will work almost automatically. If possible, change your activity in addition to changing your thoughts. For example, if you are reading, stop and go for a walk. Exercise almost always helps. Distracting yourself from the unsettling thoughts is crucial.

KEEP YOURSELF SAFE–BE AWARE

Stay safe at home, in your car, and on the streets. Lock your doors and windows. Keep lights on outside of your home or apartment at night. If you are not home before dusk use a timer and have a few of your lamps switch on before you arrive home. Don't open your door unless you absolutely know who is visiting you. Even a deliveryman may not be who he seems to be. Wait until he leaves and then retrieve your package. If someone says he is from Comcast Cable, for instance, check his credentials before opening the door and call the company. Ninety-five percent of the time a technician will not have a legitimate reason to ring your bell if unscheduled. If it is important the company will tell you so when you contact them.

Don't give out personal information of any kind to anyone you don't know. Be careful of what you write on Facebook or other social media. If you are going on vacation don't announce it to anyone but your closest friends and family.

Always wear your seat belt and don't ever drive after drinking. Don't use the phone or text while driving. If there is an emergency, pull over and make your call or text your message. If you feel too tired pull over at the nearest rest stop or safe street and rest a while. If you are alone in the car and are pulled over by the police in a deserted area call 911 and make sure the policeman is legitimate before you roll down your window. If you are stopped in a desolate area *at night* don't stop the car (go slowly with your emergency lights on) until you contact 911 and make sure the car is legitimate. At an intersection let the other driver go first if you are in the least unsure; there is no rush. Whenever you are unsure whether to go— don't! Better safe than sorry.

Try not to engage in road rage. Stay calm. You never know what crazy person you are dealing with. It's not worth it to get into an argument with a stranger or worse. Although it's important to be assertive, sometimes giving up the parking space you have been waiting for is better than a heated altercation.

When you are walking down the street, be alert. Keep your head up and don't talk on the phone or text. Make sure you know who is in front of you and occasionally check to see who is behind you. Go with your gut. If you feel funny about who is near you or approaching you, walk away or run. If there is a store nearby go in it until the person/people leave the area. Don't worry about how strangers feel or if they will be insulted. Keep this in mind when you are entering or leaving elevators.

In the mall parking lot be very aware of your surroundings. Memorize or write down where you parked your car so you don't have to wander the parking lot aimlessly. Try to park in the most crowded location so the area won't be too desolate when you return. When you leave the store take your keys out and have them ready; stay organized. Get into your car and lock it immediately, and then put on your glasses, gloves, or whatever you need in order to drive.

GO WITH YOUR GUT

If you feel it *in your gut* there is a good chance that something is going on. Go with those feelings unless at least two professionals, friends, or family members you respect suggest you do otherwise. If that is the case thoroughly research the problem and continue your deliberation. Even after weighing the issue if your feelings are very strong stick with them. Your intuition is very powerful. It can save you from making treacherous and self-defeating choices. Respect what your mind and body are communicating to you. For example, if you are about to enter a building and the person who entered before you looks menacing and your heart starts beating fast, don't enter. Wait a few minutes until he is gone. If you are walking towards your car and a group of young men are standing in front of it, and they are loud or appear suspicious, walk away for a while. Don't take the chance. If you are contemplating working with someone, but you feel that maybe he isn't quite a perfect fit, don't ignore that instinct. Think carefully whether he is really desirable as a partner. If you feel a tiny lump and you choose to ignore it for a while, but you begin feeling anxious, it is time to make an appointment with the doctor. Your body is sending you messages to take care of it. Don't ignore your body's warning signs.

DON'T ASSUME

We are not mind readers. We do not know what others are thinking unless we ask them. If you assume what others are trying to say you could get in trouble, exacerbate disagreements, and ruin relationships. If your partner, for instance, acts irritable one evening and you assume it's because he doesn't care about you, that may be completely wrong. Perhaps he had a tough day at work, or there was a lot of traffic coming home. Instead of feeling rejected or angry ask him to clarify the reason he appears cross.

DON'T MAKE MOUNTAINS OUT OF MOLEHILLS

Try not to become too dramatic, catastrophize, or make a problem or worry seem much worse than it is. Sometimes it is easy to overexaggerate a situation or concern. Attempt to be realistic and face the issue in a calm, realistic manner. In reality, there may not be that much to worry about and by keeping under control you can save yourself a lot of undue anxiety and stress. For example, if your employer speaks abstractly about the possibility of future layoffs, please don't automatically assume you will be fired and homeless. He may just be expressing some concern and have no real plan, or perhaps if it eventually happens, it will be years from now. Maybe you won't even be affected. There is no sense in worrying now while you still have the job. Another example might be if someone says something negative about you or something you perceive as negative. Maybe they were having a bad day or perhaps you misinterpreted what they said. Before you get too angry or hurt make sure the comment was actually meant for you and not someone else, and suggest the other person clarify his statement. It is easy to misunderstand what someone says or their intentions.

A young woman named Jessica had an argument with her boyfriend of two years. He was very angry and walked out of the house, slamming the door behind him. Jessica was very sensitive and interpreted her boyfriend's gesture to mean he wanted to break up. She spent the next three hours crying and full of anxiety. She was miserable and developed a migraine. She wondered if she'd ever see him again, or if she would ever meet someone she liked as much as him. Jessica went on to ponder the idea of being alone for the rest of her life. Her anguish was unwarranted because her boyfriend returned a few hours later with flowers and candy. He rushed out of the house to cool down and then realized he was in the wrong. He wanted to make it up to Jessica with the gifts and a sincere apology. Jessica had quickly jumped to the wrong conclusion. She turned a situation that was uncomfortable, but not devastating, into a tortuous experience because she was so quick to jump to conclusions.

LISTEN

Listen when others are speaking to you, especially family and close friends. Listening involves empathizing and showing the other person you hear and understand by gently nodding, maintaining good eye contact, and repeating parts of what they say from time to time. Don't work on the computer, take a phone call, or text while others are speaking. Try not to yawn or poke fun. This behavior usually makes the other person feel rejected; they may feel what they say is not important or you don't care. If you don't listen carefully you may misunderstand or misinterpret what is being said. To fully understand a message you need to observe what is actually being said, the tone of the voice, the other person's body language, and facial expressions. If you are not focusing you may miss watery eyes, a slight smile or a loving or angry gesture. Sarcasm or a sincere compliment can be quickly missed. Read between the lines; think about the message this individual is really conveying. For instance, if a wife complains that her husband doesn't love her any more and tells him to leave her alone, what she may really mean is "Show me affection; I feel hurt; I can't take your rejection and apathy anymore." She may prefer he stay, ask for forgiveness, and not leave. Don't always take things literally. Read between the lines.

GIVE THOSE CLOSE TO YOU THE BENEFIT OF THE DOUBT

Have faith in friends and family members. View them in a positive manner whenever possible. Don't jump to conclusions; believe, or at least give credence to, what they are saying as long as it is not too far fetched. Most people want to be trusted and validated. Avoid blaming and jumping to erroneous conclusions; assume the best.

BE CREATIVE

Engaging in creative endeavors helps you express feelings, thoughts, problems, fears, issues, and concerns. It helps you to become more self aware, and it enhances problem-solving skills. Creativity helps strengthen cognition, memory, and thinking. It helps create new pathways in the brain. Engaging in endeavors such as drawing helps keep you young and strong. It affords the opportunity to make choices, relax, decrease stress, and focus on the project at hand. In this way you are not ruminating or dwelling on what is wrong with your life. Art allows you to be in control and to use your unique qualities to produce works that are meaningful. It helps you to focus and be in the moment. Your mind gets the opportunity to rest and you are able to regroup. When you are creative you generally feel younger and your immune system functions more effectively. Physical and psychological pain diminishes and you feel freer. A sense of accomplishment is achieved; you have an immediate purpose. Art can be very enjoyable, stimulating, and energizing.

LIFE IS A PROCESS

Everything we experience is part of the process of life. We will have positive and negative experiences. We will succeed and we will fail. Whatever happens, one thing is certain: *there will always be change.* Nothing is permanent. If you view life as a series of experiences it will be easier to accept disappointment and easier to focus on future happiness, plans, and goals. You do not have to stay stuck in any period of your life. We almost always have the choice to move on if we choose to do so. Sometimes it is easier to stay stuck, stay a victim, but then we don't grow and enjoy life. Learn from your mistakes and do your best not to repeat them. Don't berate yourself; always forgive yourself and remember no one is perfect. Remember nothing is permanent and bear in mind the saying "This too shall pass."

DON'T LET OTHERS CONTROL YOU

If you feel strongly about something don't let yourself be persuaded to do something else by others, "Stick to your guns." It is your life and you need to be in charge. Do not live for others. There is a difference between living for others and loving and being supportive of others. The latter is normal; the former creates a loss of self-esteem and identity. Sometimes you may have to give in a little, and sometimes what you want to do is really not in your own best interest and should be changed, but most of the time follow your own path and don't let others force or manipulate you to change it.

DON'T HURT YOURSELF, HELP YOURSELF

If you are feeling stressed and/or depressed find someone supportive to speak with about your feelings. Call a hotline or 911 (999 in the UK) if you feel completely alone and hopeless. Most of the time the feeling is temporary and with the right support and medication it will change; you might very well feel much better within a few days or weeks. Have a plan ready; for example, keep phone numbers on your refrigerator of people to call when you feel desperate. Keep affirmations on the refrigerator as reminders of ways to think in a healthy manner. Create an easily accessible list of ways to distract yourself. This list may include activities such as: reading, exercise, walking, playing word and computer games, drawing, creating mandalas, watching a movie on television, listening to music, baking, cooking, browsing through old photos if they provide pleasant memories, gardening, making yourself a soothing cup of tea or hot chocolate, and journaling. Practice a mantra such as "I love my family" to say when you are troubled. Say it over and over again. Keep photos of people you love with you and look at them often.

LOVE YOURSELF

Respect yourself and demand respect from others. In most circumstances people will treat you the way you allow them to treat you. Confront someone if he is treating you poorly and don't allow abusive behavior in your life. You can be your own best friend or worst enemy. Don't label or judge yourself and don't inflict self-harm of any sort. You are too valuable to be scarred. Seek professional help and assistance from loved ones if you feel depressed, overly anxious, or hopeless. You can raise your self-esteem by valuing your self, focusing on your strengths and achievements, keeping a gratitude list and journal, being creative, helping others, exercising, and increasing positive self-talk.

NOTES

1. The CBT Triangle shows how thoughts yield feelings, which yield behavior, and *vice-versa*, and it shows how feelings can yield thoughts that yield behavior, etc. See www.adaa.org/sites/default/files/153%20Rego%20 and%20Blackmore%20Handouts.pdf for further information, accessed on 9 October 2014.

Bibliography

Buchalter, S.I. (2004) *A Practical Art Therapy.* London: Jessica Kingsley Publishers.

Buchalter, S.I. (2009) *Art Therapy Techniques and Applications.* London: Jessica Kingsley Publishers.

Buchalter, S.I. (2011) *Art Therapy and Creative Coping Techniques for Older Adults.* London: Jessica Kingsley Publishers.

Buchalter, S.I. (2013) *Mandala Symbolism and Techniques: Innovative Approaches for Professionals.* London: Jessica Kingsley Publishers.

Christensen, K., Riddoch, G.N. and Eggers Huber, J. (2009) *Dialectical Behavior Therapy Skills, 101 Mindfulness Exercises and Other Fun Activities for Children and Adolescents.* Bloomington, IN: AuthorHouse.

Greenberger, D. and Padesky, C.A. (1995) *Mind Over Mood: Change How You Feel by Changing the Way You Think.* New York: The Guilford Press.

Linehan, M.M. (1993) *Skills Training Manual for Treating Borderline Personality Disorder.* New York: The Guilford Press.

Moonshine, C. (2008) *Acquiring Competency and Achieving Proficiency with Dialectical Behavior Therapy, Volume II: The Worksheets.* Eau Claire, WI: Pesi, LLC.

Spradlin, S.E. (2003) *Don't let Your Emotions Run Your life: How Dialectical Behavior Therapy Can Put You in Control.* Oakland, CA: New Harbinger Publications, Inc.

Index

Index